Learning Science
With
Science Fiction Films

by:
Terence W. Cavanaugh
Catherine S. Cavanaugh

KENDALL/HUNT PUBLISHING COMPANY
4050 Westmark Drive   Dubuque, Iowa 52002

Learning Science With Science Fiction Films

Introduction:

Science fiction has always been a staple of motion pictures. Movie audiences have journeyed to the center of the earth and the furthest reaches of space. They have ridden in the Nautilus beneath the sea and limped around the moon and back with the crew of "Apollo 13". Spielberg alone has terrorized them with a shark and recreated the age of the dinosaur.

In many ways, the silver screen acts as a permanent ongoing science and technology exposition. Here is where most people get their regular doses of the scientific enterprise. This is good...and bad. It is good because it creates a tangible image of abstract ideas. It gives the audience a glimpse of the future and a nudge toward making it real. What effect did Georges Melies' groundbreaking 1903 film a "Trip to the Moon" have on the following generation who helped turned that science fiction into scientific reality? It is bad because good drama and good science are not always the same thing. Movies simplify and subvert scientific fact to fulfill the needs of dramatic storytelling. Undoubtedly it will take more than salt water to save humanity.

Science educators are in constant battle to change the preconceptions of students who are inspired - and confused - by the movies and television programs they see. But, these films also open a wonderful opportunity to engage the students and encourage greater understanding and interest. Consider the film "Jurassic Park". It provides educators with countless lesson opportunities. There is the question of the theoretical science within the confines of the film as well as of the practical science that went into making the special effects. It allows an opportunity to compare and contrast two drastically different eras of life on this planet. It also addresses the ethics of technological advancement. And, it's fun to watch.

The "fun" is perhaps the best weapon in a science teacher's arsenal. Science is fun and students need to see that. Too many potential scientists have been put to sleep and lost forever by the monotonous voice-overs and bland renderings that have been the hallmarks of classroom films for decades.

Fostering students' interest and excitement is crucial because the need for scientific knowledge has never been greater. It is best shown in a scene in "Apollo 13", when astronaut Jim Lovell tells a tour group at the Space Center that one day there will be a computer that can fit into a single room. Technology is racing along at warp factor six and in order to succeed in the new millennium, all students are going to need a better understanding of the sciences.

The lessons in this book are designed to help students translate what they see on the small screen into the big picture. Science is a vehicle for comprehension. It allows us to better understand ourselves and our surroundings. It teaches us how to make decisions and consider the future consequences of our actions.

Why learn science?

Scientific literacy is essential in a technological society. Everyone needs an increasing amount of science knowledge to understand changes in communication, transportation, energy, medicine, and the multitude of other rapidly developing science and technology fields.

Science is a vehicle for comprehension. Science allows us to understand ourselves and our surroundings, and changes that occur. Beyond comprehension, science provides information used in decision making.

As the world moves to an increased dependence on technology (the application of science), there will be an increase in decisions made at all levels involving scientific information and consequences. Everyone needs an understanding of science in order to participate intelligently as informed citizens in the post industrial society (National Science Foundation,

1

"Educating Americans for the 21st Century," 1983). A basic literacy in science helps in distinguishing factual media messages from pseudoscience and fallacies, creating more informed decision makers.

According to *Science for All Americans* (Rutherford & Ahlgren, 1990), science can provide humanity with the knowledge needed to develop solutions to its problems. Science encourages respect for nature that influences the use of technology. Scientific patterns of thought can help people deal with problems in all aspects of their life.

What is science fiction?

Science fiction can be described as a branch of literature in which scientific discoveries and developments form elements of plot. It is based on future prediction of scientific possibilities, some of which have become facts.

Agreement does not seem to exist on one comprehensive definition of science fiction. Science fiction seems to have different meanings, depending on whom you ask. Some very well known science fiction authors describe their genre in a variety of ways. Robert Heinlein's definition includes realistic speculation based on understanding of the scientific method. Issac Asimov's description deals with fictitious societies different from ours in technological development. Harlan Ellison's states that science fiction incorporates the future of man and science. In Theodore Sturgeon's view, human problems and solutions with scientific content are the basis around which science fiction stories are built. Damon Knight has identified common elements in science fiction including: science, technology, a distant time or place, and the scientific method. And some people even go so far as to define science fiction as anything the publishers label as science fiction.

Science fiction film differs from science fiction literature in that film focuses on the action involved in solving a problem while literature provides more of the background reason for the problem. Science fiction films often explore modern world problems and issues and provide the opportunity to consider the future and the changes that may occur. Science fiction films can be much more than just special effects, they can be the promoters of ideas and change.

Why use science fiction to teach science?

Science fiction media combine science and pseudoscience for entertainment. Science fiction television shows and movies are the strongest influences on students for promoting science, according to Purdue University research (*USA Today, The Magazine of the American Scene*, August, 1994). Interest in science can be increased and developed by science fiction. Science fiction can also help improve attitudes toward real science.

Advanced and abstract science topics such as mutations, radiation, ethics, and rocket science can be experienced by using science fiction . While hands-on direct experience is the best way to learn, often that is not possible or practical. Using science fiction allows students to experience a wide variety of science topics. Science fiction is a way for students to encounter concepts in a new context; this provides a new avenue for learning. Students are more likely to remember information they have been involved with in an entertaining or enjoyable way.

According to Dubeck, Moshier, and Boss (*Science in Cinema,* 1988), "using science films and literature to teach science can motivate a far broader spectrum of students in science than can be motivated by traditional methods." And in a recent article in the Los Angeles Times, professors and lecturers around the country use science fiction films and videos "to illustrate ideals, concepts, and scientific theories." (Delrado, 1995)

Viewing science fiction films improves learning science in various ways. The films allow direct visualization of abstract topics. High interest in science fiction facilitates learning related concepts. Discussion of science fiction films develops understanding of science processes, and the interconnectedness of science disciplines. Science fiction provides a strong motivation for learning content.

Common fallacies and errors in science fiction films

Students come to class with many preconceptions and misconceptions about science concepts. One of the sources of these mistaken beliefs is science fiction film. It is important for educators to address these misconceptions so students will not continue to believe them as facts. Teachers should be aware that their students may have misconceptions that may be supported by the film they are viewing. Teachers need to point out actual errors that occur in the film, and provide instruction to help correct the student's misconceptions.

Some of the more common fallacies that occur in science fiction films include traveling faster than the speed of light, instantaneous communication, self aware intelligent machines, gigantism, instant mutations, sound traveling in space, and the inaccurate motion of vehicles in space, just to name a very few.

Each film lesson within this book contains a partial list of scientific accuracies and inaccuracies from the film.

How to use science fiction in the classroom

The lessons included in this book are not intended to stand alone as the sole methods of teaching science concepts. The lessons are meant to enhance instruction, and seem to work best as introductory, review or interdisciplinary activities.

When used to introduce a topic, a film lesson serves as a common reference point and shared experience for the class. The film can develop the students' initial interest in a subject that may be unfamiliar. "Destination Moon" can work as an excellent introduction to the study of space travel, for example, because it shows a cartoon and live action sequences which illustrate the details involved in a moon mission.

As a concluding activity, a film lesson can provide points for discussion, reinforcement of facts learned, and a context for subject matter. Once students have the basics, they can then use the ideas from the films as areas for further research. After students have been taught about the structure of cells, for instance, they will recognize the parts encountered in the giant cell of "The Immunity Syndrome," and will be proud to point out some cell errors.

Science fiction films can also be used as the basis of an interdisciplinary activity. Students could read a book on which a film is based, or develop their own scripts, contrast societies and customs from the movie to present day, create scale models or story board representations of scenes to learn about film production and special effects, and analyze any mathematical concepts. The film "Forbidden Planet" could easily be developed into an interdisciplinary unit. The film contains a number of math and science references, uses a variety of filming techniques, contains references to Greek mythology, and is based on Shakespeare's play "The Tempest."

These films can provide an excellent core for the development of a lesson. A less formal use of a science fiction film could be to use specific film segments to illustrate a point or as an example of a concept. Teachers could also go so far as to write their own software programs using such tools as Linkway or Hypercard and a videodisc player to create interactive lessons or presentations.

How to use this book

The science fiction films and television shows used in this book have been grouped into major scientific fields. Each of the fields includes a number of fully developed self-contained lessons relating to science fiction videos. Activities and labs have been written to guide further study in the field. These labs use common household materials or items that can be easily purchased locally (a list of common chemical names and suggestions for local sources can be found on page 22). The results of these experiments can be recorded using either of the lab report formats (found on pages 20 and 21).

Each video lesson contains questions designed to be answered while watching the video. The purpose of these questions is to help the viewer follow the story and recognize scientific events as well as to develop listening skills. This process of answering the questions while watching the video makes the video segment of the lesson an active event.

Next is a list of scientific vocabulary used in the video. The vocabulary list could be presented before or after the video, in order to focus on scientific or technical terms encountered in the video. To strengthen students writing skills or to encourage students to write about science ask each student to identify three words from the vocabulary list. Each student then writes a complete sentence using one of the identified words related to their observations of that term in the video. Then repeat this process for the other selected words. After writing the sentences have another student read and critique the sentences for structure, sense, and readability. Have the student select one of the critiqued sentences to use as a topic sentence for a logical paragraph.

Discussion questions encourage further development of the scientific aspects of the film. Some lessons also have projects and activities for further research.

At the end of each topic area there are lab activities that relate to the material presented in the films of that area. While the labs are related to the film contents they are not film dependent. Labs may relate videos in several of the book's topic areas. It is not necessary or required for labs to be used with the videos in the same topic area. Lab report forms, formal and informal, are provided as a guide.

A science fiction reading list of books that contain some good accurate science facts has been developed for more experiences in learning science through science fiction.

How to get science fiction videos

Every video included in the book except "Crack in the World" can be purchased for less than $20.00 each. "Crack in the World" is not yet released on video but is often shown on the American Movie Classics cable network. Look for the films and the Star Trek® TV episodes in your local video stores, music stores, department stores, and discount stores. If the stores do not have the videos on hand, it is usually possible to order them from video sellers and renters. Tapes are also available from mail order companies such as Fusion Video (1-800-959-0061), Nostalgia Family Video (1-800-784-3362), and Critics' Choice Video (1-800-367-7765) just to name a few. If you have World Wide Web access you can also do a search for video dealers and find a number of other sources for videos.

Sample Introduction Lesson: <u>*Destination Moon*</u>

Objectives: Students will see, write about, and learn about: Space exploration and conditions, rocketry, and the physics of space using the film *Destination Moon*

Procedures:

1. Students will define and discuss the given vocabulary list.

2. Students will begin answering questions from the worksheet while watching the movie, stopping periodically for discussion as needed.

3. Once the complete film has been seen, the class will answer the mathematics/discussion question section.

4. Optional: Actual NASA footage of moon missions may be shown at this point to provide contrast.

5. A discussion of the film or a writing assignment using the discussion/essay questions.

6. Do the lab activity *Size of the Sun and Moon.*

Expected Outcomes:

Students will be able to recognize events in the film that are different from actual history.

Students will gain knowledge of conditions in space and on the moon.

Students will understand that the film is accurate in its depiction of scientific facts.

Sample Concluding Lesson : Star Trek® Cells

Objectives: Students will see, write about, and learn about: cell structures, cell functions, and immunity responses, using the "Star Trek® : Immunity Syndrome" episode.

Procedures:

Day 1: Students will define and discuss the given vocabulary list. Students will begin answering questions from worksheet while watching the episode.

Day 2: Students will complete answering questions from the episode. The class will then discuss the follow up questions.

Sample Interdiscplinary Lesson: Forbidden Planet

Science: Students will watch the film and do the related science activities included in the Learning Science with Science Fiction Films book. They will also do the lab activity *Personal Radiation Dose.*

Math: Students will do work involving calculations of speed, and learn the concepts of powers of ten. Students should also do calculations involving gravitation to determine weight.

Social Studies: Students will use the film to compare the length of exploratory voyages through history and the nature of the "frontier."

Art: Students will create their own story board representations of scenes or settings, or students will develop their own costume designs.

Language Arts: Students will study the play "The Tempest" and compare the play to the film.

Synopsis of Videos:

Feature Films   *Star Trek® TV Programs*

Andromeda Strain: A secret government research team is called into action when a satellite crashes into a town and most of the residents die. The scientists discover that a crystal (lifeform?) they call Andromeda is responsible and they attempt to devise a method to stop it from spreading. When Andromeda is accidentally released into the laboratory, the scientists must stop an atomic bomb from spreading the disease

Arena: While responding to an attack of a Federation outpost, Kirk is kidnapped and placed into a duel. In the process of the duel he finds materials to create gunpowder and construct a crude cannon, which he uses to overcome his opponent.

Beginning of the End: Radiation causes grasshoppers to mutate, becoming gigantic, and eat everything in their path as they swarm toward Chicago. The people learn that low temperatures slow the locusts, and find a sound which attracts the swarm. Sound is used to lead the insects to their deaths.

Booby Trap: While answering a distress signal, the Enterprise becomes bombarded by radiation. As more energy is put out to escape the trap, more radiation is put out to kill the crew. The crew discovers generators that convert their output energy into the lethal radiation. Using modeling systems a method is discovered to escape, by using less energy.

Crack in the World: Scientists trying to tap into a new source of power drill through the Earth's crust to reach the magma. When they are stopped by a superhard layer, they use a nuclear bomb to break through, accidentally triggering a series of earthquakes. The earthquakes, following fault lines, break through the crust, and cause a section of crust to be blown into space forming a new moon.

Day of the Triffids: People world wide are blinded by a meteor shower, and a species of plant is mutated by the radiation, causing the plants to become mobile and predacious. Marine biologists discover that seawater instantly kills the plants.

Day the Earth Stood Still: A spaceship lands in a park in Washington, D.C. A person (Klaatu) and a robot (Gort) emerge. The army, overreacting shoots the person who is then taken to the hospital. Klaatu escapes and goes out among humanity to learn about people. He enlists the aid of a local scientist in gathering scientists from around the world so that he can give them a message for humanity. To get people's attention, Klaatu stops electricity all over the world. In the end Klaatu delivers the message to live in peace or be destroyed by the robot police.

Destination Moon: Private industry takes up the challenge to make Americans the first people to set foot on the moon. After constructing and traveling in a nuclear powered rocket to the moon, the crew members find that they have used too much of their fuel. The crew strips the ship in order to lessen the ship's mass and increase their fuel efficiency to go home.

Devil in the Dark: The crew of the Enterprise, while on a mining planet, encounters a new lifeform. The silicon based (inorganic) lifeform fighting back against threats to its eggs, attempts to destroy the people. Upon discovering that the silicon lifeform is intelligent, people make a pact with it and learn to coexist.

Earthquake: 1970's disaster movie of a major Los Angeles earthquake. In the film data collected and other occurrences observed seem to lead to the prediction of an earthquake. The earthquake occurs and the story continues with the efforts of people to survive after a major earthquake.

Ethics: After an accident injures his spine, Whorf must decide on whether to risk experimental surgery or survive with limited mobility. Emotionally unable to accept limited mobility, he chooses the experimental surgery. Only his alien physiology of redundant systems allows him to survive the surgery.

Fantastic Voyage: A scientist, dying of a blood clot in the brain, holds the secret to prolonged miniaturization. A crew and submarine are miniaturized to destroy the clot. They travel through several body systems on the mission.

Forbidden Planet: A rescue ship, sent to find survivors on a distant planet, finds only two survivors. The survivors have been using the nuclear technology of a now extinct race to enhance themselves and their condition. As a side effect of using the alien technology to boost intelligence, a man's unconscious self takes form and attacks others.

Home Soil: The crew of the Enterprise visits a planet that is in the process of terraforming, when an engineer is killed under strange circumstances. An inorganic, intelligent lifeform is discovered and studied using the scientific method. A struggle ensues for control of the Enterprise between the crew and the inorganic crystal lifeform. The crew finally wins by turning out the lights.

Immunity Syndrome: The crew of the Enterprise encounters a giant cell from outside the galaxy which seems to absorb all known forms of energy. The crew, while using stimulants to counteract the energy loss, investigates and discovers that the cell is preparing to divide. The Enterprise, acting as an antibody for the galaxy, uses antimatter to destroy the cell.

It Came from Beneath the Sea: Due to atomic testing a giant mollusk must search for new food sources (people). The navy, responding to this threat, attempts to kill the giant creature with high voltage and explosive harpoons.

Jaws: A great white shark starts attacking people in a resort community during the summer holiday season. The chief of police, with an ichthyologist and a local fisherman, go out to hunt and kill the shark.

Journey to the Center of the Earth: A group of explorers enters a volcano to follow the path of a previous explorer to the center of the Earth. They encounter cave formations, lost civilizations, dinosaurs, mineral deposits, and a great underground ocean. The explorers are able to escape from the center of the Earth by using a volcanic chimney to the surface.

Jurassic Park: Scientists using DNA extracted from fossils recreate dinosaurs, which are raised on an island for a tourist attraction. Without full understanding of the problems of bring extinct species to life, people lose control of the dinosaurs and must try to escape from the park.

Monolith Monsters: A meteorite containing crystals with strange properties crashes onto the Earth. The crystals are discovered to absorb all silicates in the presence of water. The crystals, when wet, grow to giant proportions, then fall and crush anything in their path. To stop the crystals from destroying the town, a geologist discovers that the crystal growth is halted by saltwater.

Operation Annihilate: A cellular parasite controls people's nervous systems on a planet. The Enterprise crew discovers that a particular frequency of light is lethal to the parasite.

StarTrek® IV: The Voyage Home: An unknown probe heading toward the Earth attempts to communicate with a now extinct species. As a side effect of the attempt at communication, the probe is causing destruction. In order to get a whale for communication with the probe, Kirk and the crew travel back in time and bring whales to the future to save the Earth.

Them: In the desert southwest, the deaths and disappearance of people are linked to giant ants which mutated after an atomic bomb explosion at White Sands. Cyanide gas is used at the ant nest to destroy the colony, but some ants have already fled, and the military battles the new nest in L.A.

The Thing: A military pilot, crew, and the staff of a scientific research station are involved in an investigation of a spaceship crash near the north pole. A frozen alien crewmember is brought to the base, is thawed, and then escapes. The alien is found to be similar to plants, but grows on human blood. It attacks the people, who in the end kill it using electricity.

Trouble with Tribbles: A new animal called a Tribble is being sold at a spacestation. The spacestation is storing grain for use on a planet. The Tribbles begin reproducing after being fed, and soon the Enterprise and the spacestation are overrun with Tribbles. The Tribbles get into the grain storage and begin to feed. Most of the Tribbles found in the grain are dead, exposing the plot of poison grain.

Unnatural Selection: A genetically engineered lifeform at a research station causes rapid aging of its crew. The Enterprise's doctor beams aboard to help with the antidote, but is stricken with the disease. Only through the use of the transporter can the people be saved.

Index of Topics
Arranged by Title

Index of Titles
Arranged by Topic

Science in Science Fiction Reading List:

Isaac Asimov:	Asimov's Mysteries	short stories, various topics
	Caves of Steel	mystery, robotics
	A Whiff of Death	mystery, chemistry
Gregory Benford:	The Jupiter Project	Jupiter
Ben Bova	Prometheans	genetics
Lois McMaster Bujold:	Falling Free	gravity, genetics
Grant Callin:	Saturn Alia	Saturn
Arthur C. Clarke:	The Deep Range	whales, ecology
	A Fall of Moondust	moon conditions, rescue
	The Nine Billion Names of God	short stories, various topics
	Fountains of Paradise	orbits, space elevator
	Wind from the Sun	solar wind
	Islands in the Sky	space habitats
Hal Clement:	Mission of Gravity	effects of high gravity
Lester Del Rey:	Rocket Jockey	orbital dynamics
Daniel da Cruz:	Texas on the Rocks	ice/water conservation
Dr. Robert L Forward:	Future Magic	nonfiction
Pat Frank:	Alas, Babylon	FL, nuclear war
Joe Haldeman:	The Forever War	Einstein time dilatation effects
	There is No Darkness	long-term gravity effects, genetics
	Worlds	space habitats
Robert A. Heinlein:	The Man Who Sold the Moon	space, legal, moon
	Time for the Stars	time dilatation, twins
	The Moon is a Harsh Mistress	self aware machines, moon conditions, gravity dynamics
	Space Cadet	space training, rockets, orbits
	Rocket Ship Galileo	nuclear rockets, moon
Frank Herbert:	Dune	ecology, water, religions
E. Kotani & J. M. Roberts:	Between the Stars	space habitats, asteroids
Rob MacGregor:	The Crystal Skull	South/Central American cultures
Anne McCaffrey:	Dragonsdawn	genetics, chemistry
Michael McCollum:	Antares Dawn	star structures, star formations
	Thunder Strike	asteroids, comets
	The Clouds of Saturn	Saturn, density dynamics
Walter Miller:	Canticle for Leibowitz	post nuclear war
Larry Niven:	Ringworld	space habitats, engineering
	The Integral Trees	free fall habitats, biology
	The Smoke Ring	free fall habitats, biology
L. Niven & J. Pournelle:	Lucifer's Hammer	asteroid/meteor strikes Earth
Charles Sheffield:	The McAndrew Chronicles	genetics
	Web Between the Worlds	space elevator
Dana Stabenow:	Second Star	space habitats
Allen Steele:	Orbital Decay	space habitat construction
	Clarke County, Space	space habitats
Wynne Whiteford:	Thor's Hammer	asteroid strike on the Earth

Informal Lab Report Form

Title:	Name:_____
	Date: _____
	Class:_____

Purpose/Objective:

Materials:

Procedure:

Data/results:	Diagram:

Conclusion/Analysis

The Formal Lab Report

Treat experiments as though they were your own original investigations. You will find that this makes them more interesting and enjoyable and it will make your lab report writing easier. The communication skills you develop in writing good lab reports will be useful to you in any field of work you choose.

The lab report should contain the following elements:

Title Page: The title page should include the title of the investigation, your name, the date on which the experiment was performed, and the names of others who may have worked on the experiment with you.

Introduction: State the objective of the experiment. Give background information on the concept that you have investigated and discuss any theoretical considerations that are essential to understanding the experiment.

Procedure: Describe the equipment and procedures you used to carry out the experiment. Be specific, but do not go into excessive detail.

Results: This section will include your data, calculations, and graphs. The data should be presented neatly with appropriate headings. Calculations should be presented neatly and should be well organized. The equations used for the calculations are to be given regardless of whether you have used a calculator. If graphs are required for the analysis of the results, they must be neat and clearly labeled.

Discussion: In this section, you are to evaluate the significance of your results within the context of the objective stated in the introduction (include library research). For those investigations that require systematic measurements, you may find it helpful to answer the following questions in narrative form:

1. How do my results compare to published values for the quantity I measured (if there is one)?
2. What is the average uncertainty (percentage error) in my measurements?
3. What factors contributed to the value of the uncertainty?
4. What could be done to reduce the value of the uncertainty?

For those investigations that require a more qualitative approach these questions might not be needed. However factors that effected your observations should be discussed.

Bibliography: In this section you should list any and all resources that you used in doing your research. For each resource you should write the author, title, publisher, date of publication, place of publication, and pages used.

Common names and sources for chemicals

Common Name	Chemical Name	Possible Source
Alum	Aluminum potassium sulfate	Drug/Grocery Store
Ammonia	Ammonia	Drug/Grocery store
Hydrogen Peroxide	Hydrogen Peroxide	Drug/Grocery store
Laundry Bluing	Ammonium sulfate, aniline blue	Grocery store
Soda Lime	Calcium hydroxide	Hardware stores
Salt	Sodium chloride	Drug/Grocery store
Soot cleaner	Copper chloride	Hardware store
Dehumidifier pellets	Calcium chloride	Drug/Grocery store
X-Lax®	Phenolphthalein	Drug/Grocery store
Turmeric spice		Grocery store
Rubbing Alcohol	Ethyl Alcohol	Drug/Grocery store
Vinegar (clear)	Acetic Acid	Grocery store
Salt substitute	Potassium chloride	Grocery store

Proper precautions, care, and procedures should always be used in any experiment or when handling any chemical.

References

Asimov, Issac. (1953). "Social Science Fiction." *Modern Science Fiction: Its Meaning and Its Future.* ed. Reginald Bretnor. New York: Coward-McCann. 167.

DiRado, Alicia. (1995). "Boldy Going to College." *Los Angeles Times.* February 20.

Dubeck, Leroy W.; Moshier, Suzanne E.; Boss, Judith E. (1988). *Science In Cinema: Teaching Science Fact Through Science Fiction Films.* New York: Teachers College Press.

Ellison, Harlan. (1971). "Voices." *Colloquy.* May: 5.

Heinlein, Robert. (1959). "Science Fiction: Its Nature, Faults and Virtues." *The Science Fiction Novel: Imagination and Social Criticism.* Chicago: Advent. 28.

Knight, Damon. (1977). "What is Science Fiction?" *Turning Points: Essays on the Art of Science Fiction.* New York: Harper & Row. 64.

Lerner, Frederick A. (1985) *Modern Science Fiction and the American Literary Community.* Metuchen, New Jersey: The Scarecrow Press, Inc.

Manchel, Frank. (1982). *An Album of Great Science Fiction Films.* New York: Franklin Watts.

National Science Foundation. (1983). *Educating Americans for the 21st Century.* CPCE-NSF-03. Washington, D.C.

Nicholls, Peter, Ed. (1982). *The Science in Science Fiction.* New York: Crescent Books.

Rutherford, F. James; Ahlgren, Andrew. (1990). *Science For All Americans.* New York: Oxford University Press.

"That's Entertainment." (1994). *The Science Teacher.* May.

Spinrad, Norman. (1973). *Modern Science Fiction.* Garden City, New York: Anchor Books. 1-2.

Sturgeon, Theodore; Atheling, William. (1964). *The Issue at Hand.* Chicago: Advent. 14.

"How to Boost Interest in Science." (1994). *USA Today.* August 123 (2591).

Biology Human:

Fantastic Voyage
Immunity Syndrome
Unnatural Selection

Activity:
Catalyst Enzymes

FANTASTIC VOYAGE
Teacher Information

Content Areas:
Human anatomy and physiology

Synopsis:
A scientist, dying of a blood clot in the brain, holds the secret to prolonged miniaturization. A crew and submarine are miniaturized to destroy the clot. They travel through several body systems on the mission.

Good Science:
An accurate depiction of blood vessels, heart, lungs, and ear. Also factual descriptions of body functions.

Bad Science:
Impossibility of shrinking (breaks the law of conservation of mass/energy). Shortage of blood cells in the plasma. Brain was shown to be largely empty with flashes of light depicting the nerve impulses. Antibodies were shown to act much too quickly and with a specific target.

FANTASTIC VOYAGE

Directed by Richard Fleischer   *First shown: 1966*
Color,   100 minutes
Academy Award Winner: Art Direction/Set Decoration & Special Effects
Based on the book by: Issac Asimov

Questions to be answered during the video:

1. What happens during the introduction sequence?

2. What kind of injury does Benish have?

3. Why is Mr. Grant to be present at the operation?

4. CMDF stands for Combined _____ _____ Forces.

5. How long can CMDF keep things miniaturized?

6. Where will the submarine be injected?

7. What are they trying to get to in Benish's brain?

8. What body system are they using to get to the brain?

9. How small will the submarine become?

10. How will the clot be dissolved?

11. From what will the sub be in danger of attack?

12. What are Benish's "vitals"?

      Heart rate:_____   Respiration:_____   Temperature:_____

13. What can't be reduced in size?

14. Proteus is the name of _____

15. What is the sub put into after Phase I?

16. What is the problem that Dr. Micheals has?

17. Where on the body is the ship injected?

18. Why is the blood in the body not red?

19. Why does the crew feel it is too dangerous to go through the heart?

20. How does the "outside" surgical team stop Benish's heart?

21. How many times does the heart beat in a year?

22. How thick are the capillaries near the lung?

23. Where does the crew get the air for the sub?

24. What are the "rocks" found in Benish's lung?

25. What do they use to fix the laser?

26. After the Pleural Cavity, what body system do they enter?

27. What is attacking around the ship?

28. What is the danger in passing through the ear?

29. What is clogging the intake vents of the ship?

30. What does the woman do that attracts the antibodies?

31. What happens to the antibodies on the woman once she gets inside the sub?

32. Why doesn't the surgeon want to test the laser?

33. What does the clot look like compared to the rest of the brain?

34. What is going to ingest the ship?

35. What are the flashes of light going by the swimmers?

36. How do the people exit the body?

Fantastic Voyage: Vocabulary

1. Antibody	2. Capillary	3. Cavity
4. Claustrophobia	5. Clot	6. Coma
7. Corpuscle	8. Deterrent	9. Ingest
10. LASER	11. Lymphatic system	12. Miniaturize
13. Microbe	14. Plasma	15. Red Blood Cell
16. Respiratory	17. Sabotage	18. White Blood Cell
19. Turbulence	20. Crystal	

Fantastic Voyage: Discussion questions

1. What was the difference between the blue and red cells?

2. How accurate do you think the film is in its depiction of the body?

Brain   Ear   Heart   Lungs   Pleural Cavity

3. Do you think that hypothermia could be used during a surgical operation?

4. Compare your body vitals to those of Benish:

Pulse: Respiration: Temperature:

5. What do you think would actually happen to the ship after it was devoured by the white

corpuscle?

6. The film depicts nerve impluses as light, but how are nerve signals actually transmitted

through the body?

Ear Diagram: Match to the following parts
1. Anvil   2. Cochlea   3. Eardrum   4. Hammer
5. Semicircular Canals   6. Stirrup

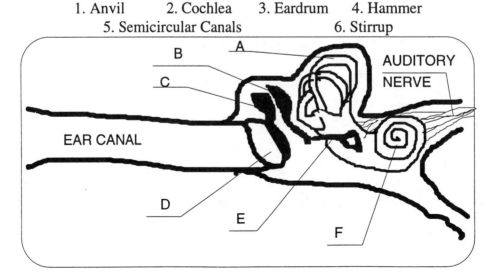

Fantastic Voyage: Answers to video questions

1. an assassination attempt
2. brain/coma
3. security
4. Miniature Deterrent
5. 60 min
6. artery
7. clot
8. circulatory system
9. approximate size of a microbe
10. laser
11. bodies' natural defenses
12. Heart: 32 beats/min; resp: 6/min; temp: 28 C
13. nuclear fuel
14. name of the sub
15. a giant syringe
16. claustrophobia
17. neck
18. plasma is clear
19. turbulence
20. electric shock
21. 40 million times
22. 1/10,000 of an inch
23. the lung
24. dust and smoke particles
25. radio parts
26. lymphatic system
27. antibodies
28. sound/vibrations
29. reticular fibers
30. damage fibers
31. they crystalize
32. prevent strain/wear out too soon
33. dark grey
34. white blood cells
35. light impulses going to the brain
36. by way of the eye

Fantastic Voyage: Suggested discussion answers

1. They are blood cells: the red cells had oxygen and the blue cells had carbon dioxide.
2. Answers will vary
3. Yes, it's used because it slows down the body systems; also slowing down deterioration.
4. Answers will vary, student results should be higher.
5. White corpuscles can't break down metals.
6. Electrochemically

Diagram:
1-B   2-F   3-D   4-C   5-A   6-E

Star Trek®: IMMUNITY SYNDROME
Teacher Information
NSTA Award winning lesson

Content Areas:
Biology, Immunity, Cell Physiology, Cell Reproduction

Synopsis:
In this Star Trek® episode the crew of the Enterprise encounters a giant cell from outside the galaxy which seems to absorb all known forms of energy. The crew, while using stimulants to counteract the energy loss, investigates and discovers that the cell is preparing to divide. The Enterprise, acting as an antibody for the galaxy, uses antimatter to destroy the cell.

Good Science:
Realistic descriptions of cell parts and processes.

Bad Science:
Impossibility of a single cell reaching huge proportions.
There is no known way to travel or communicate faster than light.
There is no known way for the transporter system to actually work.

Star Trek®: IMMUNITY SYNDROME

Episode 48 Airdate Jan. 19, 1968
Color   51 minutes
StarTrek cells and viruses

Questions to be answered during the video:

1. What does Spock say happened to the "Intrepid"?

2. Did the crew of the Intrepid know what killed them?

3. What symptoms does the crew of the Enterprise feel when entering the zone of energy?

4. What forms of matter is the "cloud" not made of?

5. As the Enterprise travels through the zone of darkness, the cloud gets stronger and the people

   on the ship get _____.

6. What does Bones say the life monitors are indicating?

7. What happened when the engines were put into reverse?

8. Why are stimulants used by the characters?

9. The interior of the object being probed consists of protoplasm.

   Its condition: _____

10. The living thing is a giant _____ animal.

11. Name one function needed to qualify something as a living organism.

12. Draw a picture of the cell from the episode

13. How does Spock know the cell is about to reproduce?

14. Where are the chromosomes?

15. For what will the chromosomes be used?

16. How is the cell affecting the Enterprise and shuttle?

17. How big is the cell in the show?

18. To what do Kirk and McCoy compare the crew?

19. What does an antibody do in a person?

20. Why does Kirk put the antimatter bomb into the nucleus of the cell?

Immunity Syndrome: Vocabulary

1. Amoeba	2. Antibody	3. Cell	4. Chromosome
5. Immunity	6. Nucleus	7. Probe	8. Protoplasm
9. Reflex	10. Reproduction	11. Stimulant	12. Symptom

Immunity Syndrome: Discussion questions

1. Compare and contrast the cell from the show to a real cell.
    What does a cell normally feed on?
    How big are normal cells?
    How do cells reproduce?

2. How does the crew know that the cell is alive?

3. Can a cell be a virus?

4. What is the difference between a plant and animal cell?
    What is the cell from the show: a plant or animal?

5. What are the problems with taking stimulants?

6. How do stimulants effect a person?

7. What factors do you feel should be considered when choosing between Spock and MacCoy to go into the cell?

8. Why is it physiologically impossible for a cell the size of the one on the show to exist on the earth?

9. Why would the explosion kill the cell?

10. Label the parts of this cell

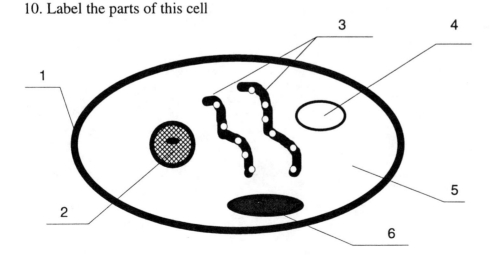

Immunity Syndrome: Answers to video questions
1. it died.
2. no
3. tired, faint, weak.
4. gas, liquid, solid.
5. weaker
6. they are all dying.
7. it went forward.
8. increase energy.
9. living
10. single-celled
11. breathe, reproduce, eat.
12. (PICTURE)
13. it has stored enough energy.
14. in the nucleus.
15. reproduction
16. draining energy
17. 11,000 miles across/(largest cell in the body is only .5 cm across)
18. antibodies, killing invasion.
19. attack an invading germ, fight infection
20. to rupture the nuclear membrane.

Immunity Syndrome: Suggested discussion answers
1. Show cell is larger, feeds off of energy instead of chemical nutrients, stores energy to reproduce.
2. Moves, responds, reproduces, eats.
3. No, viruses only contain DNA, no other cell parts.
4. Plants have cell walls and animals have cell membranes, also plants have chloroplasts. Show cell is an animal.
5. Addiction/dependence, tolerance, and physical damage.
6. Increase body and brain activity
7. Answers will vary
8. It's bigger than the Earth, and cell body couldn't withstand gravity.
9. Rupture the cell membrane.
10. Diagram:

1. Cell membrane
2. Nucleus
3. Mitochondria
4. Vacuole
5. Cytoplasm
6. Ribosomes

Star Trek the Next Generation®:
UNNATURAL SELECTION
Teacher Information

Content Areas:
Genetic Engineering, Geriatrics, Viral Infection, Adaptation/Mutation.

Synopsis:
A genetically engineered lifeform at a research station causes rapid aging of its crew. The Enterprise's doctor beams aboard to help with the antidote, but is stricken with the disease. Only through the use of the transporter can the people be saved.

Good Science:
The relationship of DNA, genes and cells is involved. The search for antibodies for a viral infection parallels present procedures. Detailed description of human aging.

Bad Science:
A person's premutation molecular pattern is revived from the transporter and used to save her. The transporter technology of beaming and reassembling matter is erroneous.
There is no known way to travel or communicate faster than light.

Star Trek: The Next Generation®
UNNATURAL SELECTION

Episode 33 Air Date 1/30/89
Color   46 Minutes
"Genes gone bad"

Questions to be answered during the video:

1. What type of message did the Enterprise receive from the Lantree?

2. What killed the crew of the Lantree?

3. What kind of organism called Thalusian flu?

4. What was the last stop of the USS Lantree?

5. What just has happened at Darwin station?

6. Research on Darwin station is limited to _____ genetics.

7. What is unusual about the physical appearance of the 12 year old child beamed aboard the

    Enterprise?

8. Why does the doctor plan to use a shuttlecraft to study they boy?

9. How does the doctor know the children carry the disease?

10. The children were designed to _____.

11. The children have genetically engineered aggressive _____.

12. The children's antibodies _____ themselves to alter the genetic code of the

    virus.

13. The children's antibodies alter the _____ of normal humans.

14. The genes that have been altered control what?

15. "Changes in evolution are caused by changes in _____"

16. Where can a DNA sample come from?

17. What kind of cells does Data use to get the doctor's DNA?

18. Scientists believe no _____ is a failure; even a _____

advances understanding.

19. Why does the Lantree's warning say keep away?

20. How does the Enterprise handle the Lantree?

Unnatural Selection: Vocabulary

1. Antibody	2. Disease	3. DNA	4. Evolution
5. Environment	6. Evolution	7. Follicle	8. Gene
9. Genetic Engineering	10. Geriatric	11. Immune System	12. Inflammation
13. Immunity	14. Quarantine	15. Risk	16. Virus

Unnatural Selection: Discussion questions

1. What do you feel are the values and risks of genetic engineering?

2. What are some real examples of adaptation and mutation?

3. Research the following Genetic Diseases:

> a. Tay-Sachs b. Down's Syndrome
>
> c. Sickle Cell Anemia d. Fragile X Syndrome
>
> e. Beta Thalassemia f. Cystic Fibrosis

4. Viral diseases such as the flu and AIDS are also constantly mutating into new forms. What are the possible consequences of being vaccinated against a virus that has a high mutation rate?

5. Bacterial diseases such as pneumonia and strep throat are mutating rapidly because of stress applied to them by antibiotics. The antibiotics kill the weaker strains of the diseases. What could be the possible consequences of widespread antibiotic use?

   What can people do to slow down this effect?

6. See if you have the following genetically inherited characteristics:

   a. Widow's Peak (hair forms a point on the forehead)

   b. Attached or Detached Earlobes

   c. The Ability to Roll or Curl the Tongue

   d. Which is the dominant thumb? (clasp hands with fingers interlaced, the dominant thumb is on top)

   e. Straight Pinky (hold little fingers next to each other and see if top joints are straight or if they point away from each other)

Unnatural Selection: Answers to video questions
1. distress signal
2. old age
3. rhinovirus (virus)
4. Darwin Genetic Research Station
5. Medical Emergency
6. human
7. looks too mature
8. isolation from people on the Enterprise
9. she gets the disease from the child by contact
10. resist diseases
11. immunity
12. adapts
13. genetic makeup
14. aging
15. environment
16. any cell
17. hair follicle
18. experiment, mistake
19. quarantine
20. blows it up

Unnatural Selection: Suggested discussion answers
1. Answers will vary.
2. Adaptation: an animal adjusting to a new food source
   Mutation: a change in the genetic structure (example cancer)
3. Answers will vary.
4. By the time the virus comes into your area it may have mutated into a new form that the vaccine is ineffective against.
5. Creation through induced selection of viruses that are not affected by antibiotics.
   To slow this effect people should use antibiotics only when necessary.
6. Answers will vary

Catalyst Enzymes

Hydrogen peroxide can be made to decompose quickly using a catalyst. A catalyst is a material that when present helps a reaction start or react faster. In this experiment we will be using a biological catalyst called **catalase**. Enzymes are biological catalysts which are made out of proteins. High temperature will destroy protein molecules. Catalase is found in many different kinds of cells. One of the places where there is a large amount of catalase is liver. Catalase is used in living cells to counteract the poisonous effects of hydrogen peroxide. Within cells hydrogen peroxide is made as a by-product of some reactions. The catalase causes the hydrogen peroxide to decompose before it can do any damage to the cell; the hydrogen peroxide breaks down into oxygen and water.

Materials:
Hydrogen Peroxide (3%)
Raw Liver (4 small pieces)
Liquid dish soap (clear works best)
4 identical drinking glasses
  (straight sides work best)
  (you can use zipper lock
    baggies instead)
Clock
Ruler

Experiment Setup

chunk liver

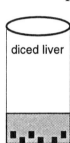
diced liver

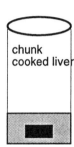
chunk cooked liver

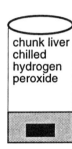
chunk liver chilled hydrogen peroxide

Procedure:
1. Cut 4 equal size pieces of liver
    (1/2 inch cubes).
2. Dice up one of the liver sections.
3. Cook one of the liver sections
    until brown (or boil 5 minutes).
4. Pour into each glass equal
    amounts of hydrogen peroxide
    (approx. 1/4 cup).
5 Chill one of the glasses of hydrogen
    peroxide until cold.
6. Add to the hydrogen peroxide in each
    glass 1 teaspoon of liquid dish soap.
7. Add liver samples into each container
    at the same time. Each glass gets one
    sample with one of the chunk samples
    going in the chilled liquid. Start timing.
    Refer to diagram
            Observe
8. At the end of two minutes
    measure how high the foam is in
    each glass.
        Record the Data

Data Table

	Chunk Liver	Diced Liver	Cooked Liver	Chunk Liver in Chilled H_2O_2
Height of Foam				

Conclusions

Give a reason for the different heights of the foam produced in each glass.

Biology Animal:

Beginning of the End
Operation Annihilate
Them

Activities:
Evidence of Speed

Acceleration Due to Gravity &
Reaction Time

BEGINNING OF THE END
Teacher Information

Content Areas:
Insect behavior, anatomy and physiology. Genetic mutation caused by radiation.

Synopsis:
Radiation causes grasshoppers to mutate, becoming gigantic, and eat everything in their path as they swarm. The people learn that low temperatures slow the locusts, and find a sound which attracts the swarm. Sound is used to lead the insects to their deaths.

Good Science:
Insect anatomy, physiology and behavior is presented factually.

Bad Science:
An insect one thousand times its natural size, and therefore 1000 times is natural weight, would not be able to structurally support itself.
Radiation is said to cause plants to grow and photosynthesize at night, as well as to cause identical mutations in hundreds of insects.

BEGINNING OF THE END

Directed by Berth I. Gordon   *1957*
Black and White   *80 minutes*
Starring Peter Graves
Giant grasshoppers invade Illinois.

Questions to be answered during the video:

1. Why does police Car 254 pull over and call in?

2. What has happened to Ludlow?

3. What kind of job does Audrey Aims have?

4. What was the town of Ludlow's population?

5. While there are no atomic installations in the local area, who is using radioactive materials?

6. What is different about the plants at the experimental station?

7. Why did Frank become a deaf-mute?

8. What animal is being picked up that got into the plants?

9. What can't the isotopes do at the experimental research station?

10. What does Ed say that the radiation is causing photosynthesis to do?

11. When was the warehouse destroyed?

12. What is it that Frank notices about the ground?

13. What kind of scientist is Ed?

14. Plants and _____ are interdependent and can't live without each

     other.

15. What happens to Frank?

16. What does Ed say is responsible for the destruction?

17. What kind of sound do grasshoppers make?

18. What convinces Ed that there are more than a few hundred giant grasshoppers?

19. What on the giant grasshoppers, or locusts, failed to develop?

20. What do grasshoppers use to communicate?

21. Toward what city are the locusts headed?

22. How effective are insecticides on the locusts?

23. When do locusts send out a high pitch screech?

24. How many legs does a locust have?

25. Why did the locusts stop their advance?

26. What happens to locusts if they spend 24 hours at 15°F?

27. Why does Ed need a live giant grasshopper?

28. How will Ed know when he has the right sound?

29. Why does the amplifier/speaker need to be on a tall building?

30. What is attracting the locusts?

31. Why does Ed need to hold out longer?

32. What happens to the locusts?

Beginning of the End: Vocabulary

1. Amplifier   2. Botanist   3. Dormant
4. Entomologist   5. Frequency   6. Hibernating
7. Insecticide   8. Isotope   9. Locust
10. Oscilloscope

Beginning of the End: Discussion questions

1. Using a science book with a picture of a grasshopper, label these parts:

    a. thorax   b. head   c. abdomen
    d. antenna   e. legs   f.. wings
    g. eyes   h. mouth

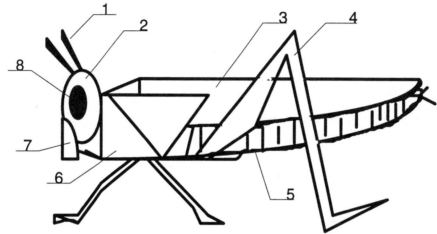

2. What would be the physical structural problems with a grasshopper that got as large as the ones in the movie?

3. The movie mentioned the interdependence between plants and insects:
    In what way do plants depend on insects?
    In what way do insects depend on plants?

4. Would exposure to radioactive substances cause a large group of animals to all mutate in the same way?

5. Is it logical to assume that what makes plants grow larger would make animals grow larger?

6. In the movie the grasshoppers were attracted to their deaths by man made sounds; animals are affected by sounds (ex. in nature grasshoppers use sound to attract mates). For each of the following give an example of how <u>people</u> control animals with sound.
    a. fleas
    b. dogs
    c. horses
    d. whales (dolphins)
    e. mosquitoes

Beginning of the End: Answers to video questions

1. they find the wrecked car
2. the town was destroyed
3. journalist/newspaper reporter
4. 150 people
5. US Department of Agriculture research station
6. they are very large (giant)
7. accident with radiation
8. snails
9. explode
10. continue night and day
11. a month ago
12. it is barren, no life
13. an entomologist
14. insects
15. he gets eaten
16. giant locust (grasshoppers)
17. clicking/chirping
18. the sound that the grasshopper made
19. wings
20. hind legs
21. Chicago
22. they are not effective/no effect
23. before they attack
24. 6
25. the temperature dropped below 68°F, it got too cold and they became dormant
26. they die
27. to experiment with
28. by the reaction of the locust
29. to have the greatest range
30. speakers on the roof
   (sound of a specific frequency)
31. to attract all of the locust from the surrounding areas
32. they enter the lake and drown.

Beginning of the End: Suggested discussion answers

1. Diagram   1-D   2-B   3-F   4-E   5-C   6-A   7-H   8-G
2. Inability to get enough oxygen, body structure couldn't support the weight, exoskeleton needs to molt and without the support the body would collapse.
3. Some plants depend on insects for pollination, dispersal of seed and defense. Insects depend on plants for food and shelter.
4. No. Cells would mutate in random ways.
5. No. Plant and animal genes are different so they would mutate differently.
6. a) ultrasonic insect repellent   b) calling and controlling with whistles
   c) can respond to verbal commands d) calling and controlling with whistles
   d) ultrasonic insect repellent

Star Trek®: OPERATION ANNIHILATE
Teacher Information

Content Areas:
Human nervous system, types of light, experimentation, parasite-host relationship

Synopsis:
A cellular parasite controls people's nervous systems on a planet. The Enterprise crew discovers that a particular frequency of light is lethal to the parasite.

Good Science:
Generation and measurement of light are discussed in detail.
Accurate description of the nervous system.
Explanation of parasitic behavior.

Bad Science:
There is no known way for a matter transporter system to work.
There is no known way to travel or communicate faster than light.
Giant parasitic nerve cells can communicate with each other without contact.

Star Trek®:
OPERATION--ANNIHILATE

Episode 29 Airdate April 13, 1967
Color   51 minutes
Star Trek® and Parasites

Questions to be answered during the video:

1. What pattern of behavior is destroying civilizations?

2. Where is the Devonian ship going?

3. What did the Devonian say as his ship burned?

4. Where are the mines located that the freight ships visit?

5. What does Sam do for a living?

6. What is wrong with the people's nervous systems while they are asleep?

7. What is wrong with Sam?

8. Both Sam's wife and child are suffering from _____

9. When did the things come?

10. Why is Sam's wife having trouble answering questions?

11. What kind of sound was Spock going to investigate?

12. Describe the alien:

13. What did the creature do to Spock's back?

14. Where is alien tissue growing in Spock's body?

15. The doctor says that the creature leaves a _____ which then grows throughout the

    body.

16. What does Spock try to do?

17. Why does Spock return to the planet surface?

18. What is the creature?

46

19. The doctor can't find something that _____ kill the creature, _____ killing the host person.

20. Stars or suns do the following: emit heat and radiation, have mass and gravity, change matter to energy, and _____.

21. What unit of light measurement is used to describe the brightness of the light?

22. What kills the creature?

23. What does the bright light do to Spock?

24. What kind of light kills the creatures?

25. Spock has _____ (like a snake) that protects him from light.

Operation--Annihilate: Vocabulary:
1. Host   2. Nervous system   3. Neuron
4. Parasite   5. Puncture   6. Sedated
7. Spectrum   8. Tranquilizer   9. Ultraviolet
10. Wound

Operation--Annihilate: Discussion questions
1. Look for information on local parasites (and side effects/problems/diseases).
   Describe how these organisms are parasites:
   a. mosquito
   b. ticks
   c. fleas
   d. ringworm fungus
   e. tapeworm
   f. virus
   g. bacteria (some forms)

2. What are the colors of the spectrum that we can see? List them in order and add ultraviolet and infrared.

3. How does ultraviolet (UV) light affect people?

4. The nervous system is made of cells called NEURONs. Look up a drawing of a neuron and label these parts:
   a. axon   b. cell body   c. dendrite   d. synapse

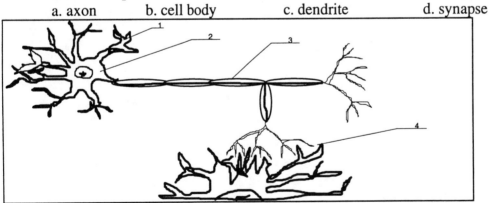

5. What do you think should have been done to the "infected" people if a cure had not been found?

Operation--Annihilate: Answers to video questions
1. mass insanity
2. the sun
3. "I did it, I'm finally free"
4. asteroid belt
5. research biologist
6. being violently stimulated
7. he is dead
8. extreme pain
9. 8 months ago
10. something is exerting pain
11. buzzing
12.
13. puncture wound
14. on his nervous system
15. stinger
16. take the ship
17. to get a creature for study
18. a single cell resembling a brain cell
19. will/not
20. emit light
21. 1,000,000 candles
22. light
23. blinds him
24. ultraviolet light
25. an inner eyelid

Operation--Annihilate: Suggested discussion answers
1. local effects will vary
    a. females feed on the blood of other animals   encephalitis
    b. ticks feed on blood   lyme disease
    c. fleas feed on blood   flea anemia
    d. ringworm grows and feeds on skin   skin problems
    e. tape worms take nutrients from host's intestine   malnutrition
    f. viruses use other living cells to reproduce   flu
    g. some bacteria use other plants and animals as food sources   infection
2. (Infrared)-red-orange-yellow-green-blue-indigo-violet-(ultraviolet)
3. Causes tanning, sunburn and skin cancer
4. Diagram: 1-C   2-B   3-A   4-D
5. Answers will vary

THEM
Teacher Information

Content Areas:
Insect colony behavior and anatomy, genetic mutation caused by atomic radiation, pest control.

Synopsis:
In the desert southwest, the deaths and disappearance of people are linked to giant ants which mutated after an atomic bomb explosion at White Sands. Cyanide gas is used at the ant nest to destroy the colony, but some ants have already fled, and the military battles the new nest in L.A.

Good Science:
Factual discussion of structure and processes of ants and ant nests.
The anatomy of ants and uses of formic acid is correct, as well as the ant's organized fighting behavior.

Bad Science:
An insect exoskeleton would be unable to support its weight if it was 10 feet long, and its respiratory system couldn't supply enough oxygen.
Ants would not be incapacitated by the loss of antennae.
Some ants are resistant to cyanide.

THEM

Directed by: Gordon Douglas *1954*
Black and White *93 minutes*

Questions to be answered during the video:

1. The movie begins in what state?

2. How does the little girl act?

3. How do you know an ordinary robbery has not happened at the trailer?

4. What do the police find on the ground outside the trailer?

5. What makes the little girl react?

6. What similarities are there between the evidence at the trailer and at the store?

7. What kind of acid could have killed "Gramps"?

8. When and where did the first atomic bomb explode?

9. What does the little girl say?

10. Where on the body should goggles be worn?

11. What kind of doctor is Dr. Medford?

12. How big is the footprint?

13. From the size of the footprint, how big is the animal that made it?

14. What makes the whistling sound and prints?

15. The ant is helpless without which part?

16. What caused the ant mutation?

17. How do ants kill?

18. What was the purpose of the ant sound?

19. Why weren't the ants seen before?

20. List the parts of an ant mound.

21. How do ants breathe?

22. What two chemicals are used to trap and kill the ants?

23. Does the hydrogen cyanide gas sink in the presence of air?

24. With what material are the ant mound walls held together?

25. What hatched from the empty egg case?

26. What distinguishing feature do queen ants have?

27. How do ants smell, feel and sense (with what)?

28. Ants can lift how many times their own weight?

29. When do male ants die?

30. How long can a queen lay eggs after one mating?

31. What behaviors do ants and man have in common?

32. Where did the USS Viking pick up its ants?

33. How much sugar did the Los Angeles ants steal?

34. Where do the Los Angeles ants live?

THEM: Vocabulary

1. Acid	2. Antenna	3. Atomic bomb
4. Density	5. Drone	6. Entomologist
7.Mutate	8. Queen	9. Radiation

THEM: Discussion questions

1. What things did the ants do that giant ants wouldn't really be able to do?

2. The giant ants are called mutants by the scientists. What is a mutant?

    What are mutations?

    Can radiation cause mutations?

    Can an atomic bomb cause mutations?

3. Do you think an insect exoskeleton could support the body of a giant ant?

    Could giant ants breathe well enough to get oxygen to all of their cells?

4. Does the film portray a realistic danger in the atomic age?

    What are more realistic dangers?

5. Why do x-ray technicians and patients wear lead protection?

6. Do you think the Drs. Medford are believable characters?

    Are either of them a stereotype?

7. What is the gram formula weight of hydrogen cyanide (HCN)?
        What is the gram formula weight of air (remember its mostly N_2)

THEM: Answers to video questions

1. New Mexico
2. dazed, shocked, and nonresponsive
3. the money was left
4. prints/marks on the ground
5. whistling noise
6. walls broken down and money not taken
7. formic acid
8. White Sands, New Mexico, 1940's
9. Them!!
10. over the eyes
11. an entomologist
12. over 12 cm
13. over 8 ft. (2.5 m)
14. radiation
15. antennae
16. radiation (from atomic bomb)
17. injection of formic acid
18. communication
19. lived in the desert
20. entrance, food chambers, Queens chamber, nursery, tunnels, water traps, and farms.

21. through their sides
22. phosphorus and cyanide gas
23. yes
24. saliva
25. queens
26. wings
27. antennae
28. 20 times
29. after mating
30. for life
31. make war
32. Acapulco, Mexico
33. 40 tons
34. sewers

THEM: Suggested discussion answers

1. Move about, fly
2. A mutant is anything that has undergone a genetic mutation. A mutation is a change in DNA structure. Radiation can cause mutation. An atomic bomb could cause mutations because of its large output of radiation.
3. The structure of the skeleton could not support the mass of the giant ant. Also the ant's breathing tube system would not allow oxygen to diffuse fast enough to the body cells.
4. Answers will vary. Insect mutation of this type is not a real danger. A more realistic danger could be the formation of a new virus, contamination due to radioactive waste, radiation sickness.
5. The lead is very dense matter which shields the body from some forms of radiation.
6. Answers will vary, but yes, they are stereotypes.
7. HCN = 27 grams per mole
   N_2 = 28 grams per mole

Evidence of Speed

It's possible sometimes to gather information from indirect evidence about an animal. The footprint of an animal may tell many things. A biologist named R. McNeill Alexander developed a formula to calculate the speed of a living animal from the trackways (series of footprints) that the animal left behind. His formula used the stride distance and hip height to calculate the speed.

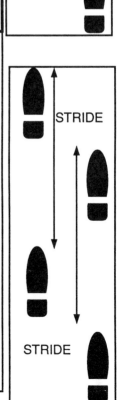

Materials
Scientific Calculator
Meter Stick
Timer
Place to walk or run
    where foot prints
    show

A TRACKWAY can be divided into three sections: The PACE, the distance between the right and left foot; the STRIDE, the distance between two successive steps (right-right, or left-left); and the GAUGE, which is the width of the tracks, telling how close the legs were together. Measure toe to toe.

Procedures:
1. On sand (or other good footprint area) measure out 5 meters.
2. Walk or run across this area timing how long it takes to go the 5m.
3. Measure your foot length and multiply by 4 to get the hip height.
4. Measure your stride from the footprints.
5. Calculate your speeds (on data table below).
6. Compare the two methods of calculation.

Data Table:

Distance covered .... 5_____meters

Time ...._____seconds

Measured Speed = $\dfrac{\text{distance}}{\text{time}}$ =
    _____meters/second

Foot Length = ..._____meters

Hip Height (4 times foot length) = ..._____meters

Pace Length = ..._____meters

Stride Length = ..._____meters

Formula for direct measurement:

speed = $\dfrac{\text{distance}}{\text{time}}$ =
    ...._____meters/second

Formula for Indirect measurement: (Alexander's)

speed= $\dfrac{(.25\ g)^{0.5}(\text{stride})^{1.67}}{(\text{hip height})^{1.17}}$ =
    ...._____meters/second

Acceleration Due to Gravity
& Reaction Time

Since gravity is always pulling down on objects, there is a constant force. This constant force causes a constant acceleration on falling bodies (up to terminal speed). The formula to find out how far an object has fallen during a time is **distance=1/2 acceleration due to gravity times time squared (d=½gt²)**. Near the Earth's surface the acceleration due to gravity is 32 feet/sec² or 9.8 meters/second² or 980 centimeters/second². We can also use this information to find out your reaction time. Reaction time is the amount of time it takes you to react and respond to a situation.

Procedure
1. Cut out the strips on the other page, tape together and tape a penny as a weight on the bottom.
2. Have someone hold the paper strip with the start between your thumb and first finger, holding your fingers two to three inches apart next to the start mark.
3. When they drop the paper try to catch it. The time on the tape where you catch it is your reaction time.
4. Record your data.
5. Try the experiment with your right hand, your left hand and your feet.
6. Try the experiment on someone else.
NOTE: the experiment will only work if someone else drops the tape.

Data Table						
	Person #1			Person #2		
Test	Left Hand	Right Hand	Both Feet	Left Hand	Right Hand	Both Feet
1						
2						
3						
Average						

Questions:
1. Is there any difference between your left and right hand? If so why?.
2. Why do you suppose that there is a difference between hands and feet?(what reason)
3. If you drop a rock off a bridge and the rock hits the water 3 seconds later how high is the bridge?

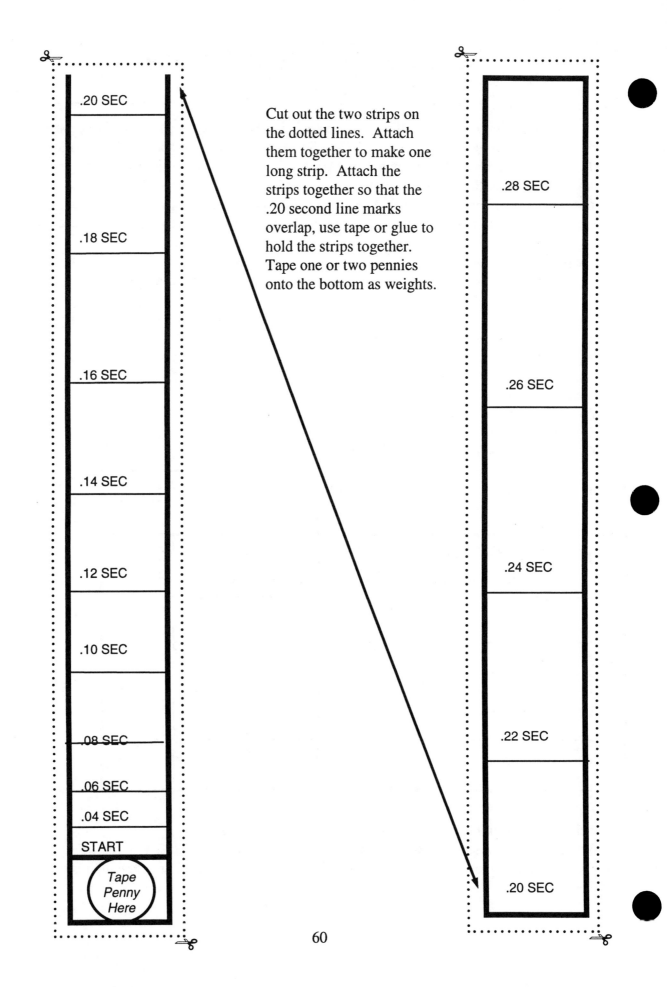

.20 SEC

.18 SEC

.16 SEC

.14 SEC

.12 SEC

.10 SEC

.08 SEC

.06 SEC

.04 SEC

START

Tape Penny Here

Cut out the two strips on the dotted lines. Attach them together to make one long strip. Attach the strips together so that the .20 second line marks overlap, use tape or glue to hold the strips together. Tape one or two pennies onto the bottom as weights.

.28 SEC

.26 SEC

.24 SEC

.22 SEC

.20 SEC

60

Biology Plant:

Day of the Triffids
The Thing

Activities:
Flower Dissection,
Build a Flower

DAY OF THE TRIFFIDS
Teacher Information

Content Areas:
Plant anatomy, tropisms, reproduction, forms of energy, and uses of technology.

Synopsis:
People worldwide are blinded by a meteor shower and a species of plant is mutated by the radiation, causing the plants to move and become predacious. Marine biologists discover seawater instantly kills the plants.

Good Science:
Plants do have limited motion and carnivorous capabilities. The film shows a true relationship between plants and animals when it describes plants getting nutrients from animal waste and remains.

Bad Science:
A meteor shower triggers no harmful radiation, and the shower would not be visible world wide at the same time. Also the mutation would not affect all the people/plants identically. Seawater should not dissolve a lifeform that has saline fluids inside, like most life on Earth.

Other Information:
You can usually purchase Venus Fly Traps at local garden centers or greenhouses, to use as examples of carnivorous plants.

DAY OF THE TRIFFIDS

Directed by Steve Sekely   1963
Color   93 minutes
Based on the book: The Day of the Triffids *by John Wyndham*

Questions to be answered during the video:

1. What type plant is shown in the opening scenes eating insects?

2. What kind of shower is occurring?

3. What happens to the Triffids during the shower?

4. Why can't Mansen watch the shower?

5. What is Tom's occupation?

6. What does the girl want to dissect?

7. How do the Triffids move?

8. What happens when the Triffids scratch the guard?

9. What causes Mansen to take off his bandages?

10. Why is Dr. Soons blind?

11. The Triffids can inflict what kind of sting?

12. What are the people afraid might occur in the train station?

13. Why does the large man want the little girl?

14. What did the Triffid appear to do at the car?

15. Who is Mansen trying to get in contact with?

16. What is Tom going to use to kill the plant?

17. Where did the plant go?

64

18. How does Tom apparently kill the Triffid?

19. What does Mansen think will happen in France?

20. Tom says "All plants _____."

21. What happened to the Triffid Tom "killed"?

22. What do Mansen and Kocker find while getting food?

23. How do Triffids reproduce?

24. From where did the Triffids come?

25. What does the crashed pilot say?

26. What happened at the chateau while Mansen was gone?

27. Why does she feel guilty?

28. What acid has no effect on Triffids?

29. What did Mansen put up to keep out the Triffids?

30. When there is not enough power to keep the Triffids out, what does Bill do?

31. To what are the Triffids attracted?

32. What kind of ship's crew picks up Mansen?

33. What does Tom discover that kills Triffids?

Day of the Triffids: Vocabulary

1. Astronomer	2. Auxiliary	3. Barricade	4. Botanist
5. Botany	6. Carnivore	7. Cortex	8. Dissect
9. Dissolve	10. Fatal	11. Generator	12. Glare
13. Meteor	14. Optic	15. Pestilence	16. Pupil
17. Regenerate	18. Tissue		

Day of the Triffids: Discussion questions

1. How are plants and animals named? What do you think the name triffidus celestis means?

2. Is it reasonable to expect that all the world could go blind at the same time?

3. Why were the convicts not blind?

4. How could the Triffids hear?

5. What problems do you think would occur if a large percent of a population went blind?

Mini project:

Break the class down into three groups. Each group will do a mini report and make a picture of
    one of the following carnivorous plants. Each mini report should include where in the
    world the plant is found, what environment it lives in, what the plant eats, how it attracts
    or catches its food, and any other major plant characteristics.

1. The Venus Fly Trap	4. The Waterwheel Plant
2. The Pitcher Plant	5. The Bladderwort
3. The Sundew	6. The Butterwort
a. Narrowleaf c. Spoonleaf	
b. Roundleaf d. Threadleaf	

Match each of the following to the parts of the flower:
    1. Ovary with seeds   2. Petals   3. Pistils   4. Sepals   5. Stamen with pollen

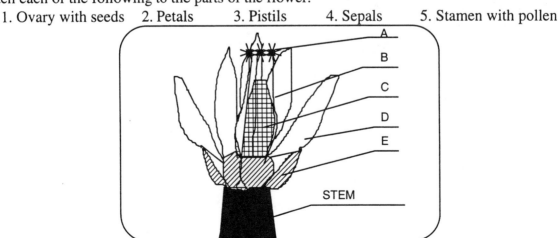

Day of the Triffids: Answers to video questions

1. Venus Fly Trap
2. meteor shower
3. they grow larger
4. eye operation/has bandages on
5. marine biologist
6. stingray
7. roots pull them across the ground
8. turns green and dies
9. he hears the bell ring 9 am/hears a scream
10. glare from watching the meteor shower
11. fatal
12. fire or accidents
13. because she can see
14. spit
15. other sighted people / disaster meeting in
    Paris
16. a harpoon
17. inside the lighthouse
18. cuts off the flower
19. fire, starvation, pestilence
20. move
21. escaped/regenerated
22. a field of Triffids
23. seeds carried with the wind
24. meteors
25. a rescue center
26. convicts took over
27. she survived
28. nitric
29. an electric fence
30. burns them
31. sound
32. submarine
33. salt water

Day of the Triffids: Suggested discussion answers

1. Plants and animals are named with Latin names that describe them or may be named after their
    discover.
    Triffids from the stars (or space)
2. Only if the meteors were bright enough to be seen during the day
3. They were not able to watch the meteor shower while in prison.
4. There are theories that some plants can sense sound but the method is unknown.
5. Answers will vary
Diagram
1-C   2-D   3-B   4-E   5-A

THE THING
Teacher Information

Content Areas:
Plant anatomy, metabolism, reproduction, and physiology, arctic conditions, radiation detection, and radar.

Synopsis:
A military pilot, crew, and the staff of a research station are involved in an investigation of a spaceship crash near the north pole. A frozen alien crewmember is brought to the base, and is thawed and then escapes. The alien is found to be similar to plants, but grows on human blood. It attacks the people, who in the end kill it using electricity.

Good Science:
Factual depiction of arctic conditions, plant survival and regeneration capabilities, and use of scientific instruments like compasses and Geiger counters.

Bad Science:
The alien plant didn't seem to need light for photosynthesis, and didn't alter its activity level in varying temperatures.

Other Information:
You can see phototropism (movement due to light) in plants if you allow a potted leafy plant to sit near a window for a few days, notice the orientation of the leaves, and then turn the plant around. Over the next few days (or that day depending on the plant) you should be able to observe the leaves changing orientation.

THE THING, FROM ANOTHER WORLD

Directed by Christian Nyby   1951
Black and White   87 minutes
Based on the Story "Who Goes There?" by Joseph Campbell
(What not to say when a plant walks up and knocks you down)

Questions to be answered during the video:

1. In what state does the story begin?

2. Where is the research station that reported an unusual plane crash?

3. When the crew get off the plane what form of transportation do they use?

4. Who (what famous explorer) went to the North Pole once?

5. Name an instrument that registered a disturbance:

6. The object hit the ground with an impact of _____ tons of steel.

7. What instrument is being used to evaluate the crash item?

8. What is the shape of the craft?

9. After the explosion what kind of reading does the crewman get with his Geiger counter?

10. Name one of the three reasons that the Air Force stopped investigating UFO's:

11. Why did the <u>scientist</u> **not** want the THING exposed to the air?

12. While the arm from the THING has a chitinous substance which was amazingly strong, what
    did the arm **not** have?

13. The scientists say that the THING is composed of what type matter?

14. What plant on Earth can send messages to others of its type far away?

15. What kind of pods were found in THING's hand?

16. What was the reason given for the hand becoming alive again?

17. What did the THING need that could only be found in the greenhouse?

18. When the doctor planted the THING's seeds, what did he add to them to make them grow?

19. How did the THING heal itself after losing its arm?

20. Which of the Doctor's planted seeds grew best?

21. What method does the crew decide to use to kill the THING?

22. What is the temperature outside the station?

23. What form of energy is finally used to kill the THING?

WARNING: Watch the skies everywhere!

THING: Vocabulary

1. Artery	2. Chitin	3. Evolution
4. Geiger counter	5. Generator	6. Greenhouse
7. Hysteria	8. Magnetometer	9. Plasma
10. Radiation	11. Tissue	12. Trace (noun)

THING: Discussion questions

1. Label the parts of the plant cell:

1. Cell Wall	2. Chloroplasts	3. Cytoplasm
4. Endoplasmic Reticulum	5. Mitochondrion	6. Nucleolus
7. Nucleus	8. Vacuole	

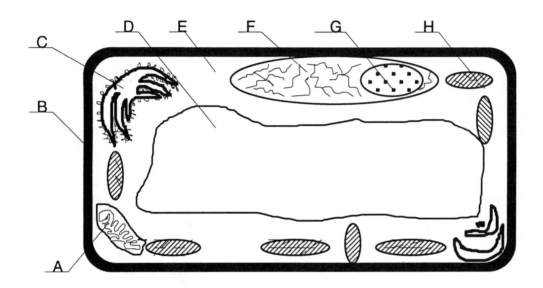

2. How is a plant different from an animal?

3. If plants have no nerve cells how could they "sense" their surroundings?

4. How do plants respond to their surroundings?

5. Give three examples of plant movement:

6. How could plants communicate with each other?

THING: Answers to video questions
1. Alaska
2. north pole
3. dog sled
4. Peary
5. compass/seismograph/magnetometer
6. 20,000
7. geiger counter
8. round
9. trace
10. no evidence, mass hysteria, they are jokes
11. don't know what organisms are present or how Earth air will effect it.
12. blood, animal tissue, arterial structure, nerve endings
13. plant/vegetable
14. telegraph vine
15. seed pods
16. ingested canine blood
17. soil
18. blood/plasma
19. it grew a new one
20. the ones near the food source
21. burn it
22. -60°F
23. electricity

THING: Suggested discussion answers
1. 1-B 2-H   3-E   4-C   5-A   6-G   7-F   8-D
2. Plant cells have cell walls and animal cells have cell membranes, plants have chloroplasts, plants take in carbon dioxide, and plants make their own food.
3. Plants have tropisms, responses to gravity and light, for example.
4. Leaves grow toward sunlight, roots grow toward gravity.
5. Growth, following sunlight, Venus fly traps closing.
6. Chemical signals, electrical signals, answers will vary.

Flower Dissection

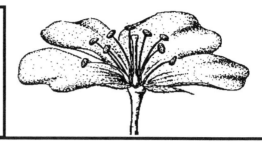

Materials:
Large flower (such as tulip, gladiolus, lily...)
Hand lens or magnifying glass
Small sharp scissors
Colored pencils or crayons
Clear cellophane tape

The flower is the main reproductive part of an *angiosperm* (flowering plant). A <u>perfect</u> flower contains both male and female parts, an <u>imperfect</u> has only one sex present. The female, egg-producing part is the *pistil*, made of the *stigma*, *style*, and *ovary*. The male sperm-producing part is the *stamen*, composed of the *anther* and *filament*.

The bright colors and strong scents of flowers attract insects, birds and other animals which move *pollen* from *stamen* to *pistil*, so fertilization can take place. Other flowers pollinate by wind and are usually not brightly colored (brown or green) or strongly scented, and the *anthers* of these flowers tend to dangle out of the flower, so they can be caught and moved by the winds.

Diagram your flower in the space provided and label each of the following parts, checking them off as you go.

1.___ **Sepal** - find the green leaf-like structure at the base of the flower where the petals attach to the stem. The sepal surrounds the flower before it opens.

2.___ **Petal** - locate the large, colorful parts inside the sepals surrounding the internal reproductive parts.
   How many petals does the flower have? _____
   the number can be used to determine whether the flower is a monocot or a dicot. Monocots have 3 petals, and dicots have 4, 5, or multiples of 5 petals.

3.___ **Stamen** - remove the petals from the flower and look at the long/thin structures with sacs at the top, these stamens surround the central stalk of the flower.

4.___ **Filament** - this part is the long, thin supporting section of the stamen.

5.___ **Anther** - at the top of a filament is the anther - where dusty pollen grains are located. Each pollen grain contains sperm cells. Collect some pollen grains on a 1 inch piece of tape and tape down onto the labeled section.

6.___ **Pistil** - the central stalk in the flower is the pistil. Remove the stamens, and carefully use a sharp tool to cut lengthwise down through the pistil to see the inside.

7.___ **Stigma** - the top if the pistil is the stigma, this place receives pollen from the anther.

8.___ **Style** - the style is below the stigma, pollen tubes lead down from the stigma to the ovary.

9.___ **Ovary** - the ovary is the base of the pistil where eggs are located. When the eggs are fertilized by sperm, they become seeds.
What part of a plant usually contains seeds? _____

Fill in the following chart.

Flower Part Name	Male	Female	Description	Function
1. Sepal				
2. Petal				
3. Stamen				
4. Filament				
5. Anther				
6. Pistil				
7. Stigma				
8. Style				
9. Ovary				

Draw, color and label
your flower here ⟶

Pollen Sample ↓

Build a Flower

Flowers are the reproductive organs of angiosperms, or flowering plants. Angiosperms make up the largest group of plants in existence. In flowers reproduction is a multi- stage process. First pollen must be transferred, then sperm from the pollen travels down to the ovule, causing fertilization to occur. The fertilized egg in the flower develops into a seed and then into a fruit.

In this activity you will make a model flower. Use your model to help identify the parts of actual flowers.

Instructions:

1. Color both sides of each picture

2. Cut out each picture

3. Roll F around a pencil and glue into a tube. Spread out the top.

4. Glue leaves G (bottom only not actually leaves) around tube F

5. Glue H into a tube and insert into bottom of F

6. Glue A onto B, B onto C, C onto D, D onto E

7. Fold A-D up and fold E down

8. Glue A-E onto top of F

COLORING KEY

1 =GREEN	
2 =RED	
3 =BROWN	
4 =YELLOW	

cut — · — · — · — ·

Note: not all flowers contain all parts.

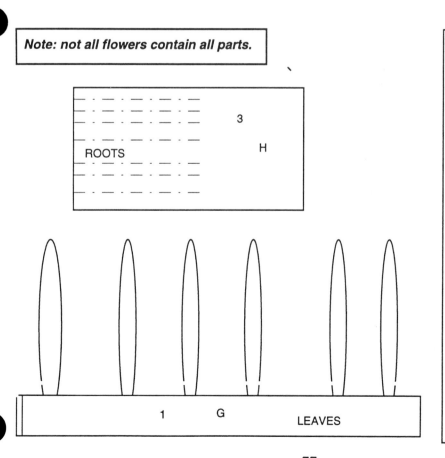

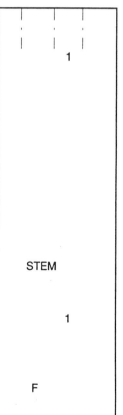

77

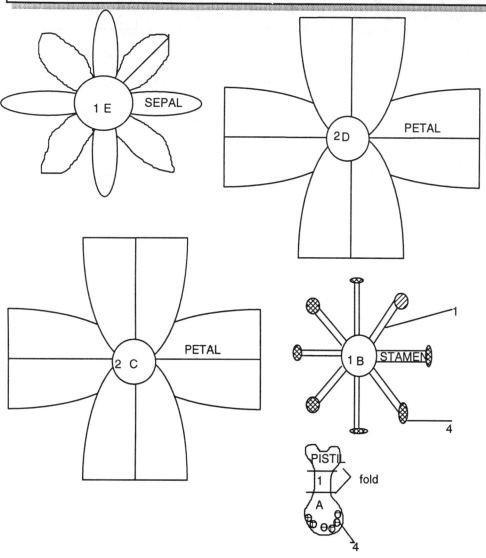

1 E   SEPAL

2D   PETAL

2 C   PETAL

1B   STAMEN
1
4

PISTIL
1   fold
A
4

assembly diagram

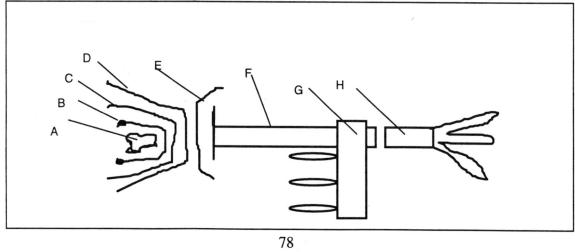

D
C
B
A
E
F
G
H

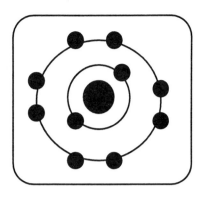

Chemistry:

Andromeda Strain
Arena
Home Soil

Activities:
Conductivity Tester,
pH & Indicators,
Crystal Growth

THE ANDROMEDA STRAIN
Teacher Information

Content Areas:
Biological warfare, infection, biosafety, scientific method, biochemistry, pH, mutation, satellite technology.

Synopsis:
A secret government research team is called into action when a satellite crashes in a town and most of the residents die. The scientists discover that a crystal (lifeform?), they call Andromeda, is responsible and they attempt to devise a method to stop it from spreading. When Andromeda is accidentally released into the lab, the scientists must stop an atomic bomb from spreading the disease.

Good Science:
Scientific procedures used to isolate the disease, the methods of determining its size and vector (method of transfer) are accurate.
The biosafety procedures.
All of the human physiology presented.
The portrayal of the epileptic seizures.

Bad Science:
The birds in the town should have been dead, just like the people, dogs and cats.
The decontamination procedure used to clean the suits on the scientists would not have worked on Andromeda, since radiation would have caused it to grow.

THE ANDROMEDA STRAIN

Directed by Robert Wise   First shown 1971
Color   130 minutes
Based on the book The Andormedia Strain by Michael Crichton
(Germs from space?)

Questions to be answered while watching the video

FIRST DAY

1. What are the Air Force personnel going to Piedmont to get?

2. What do the Air Force personnel and the pilot see in town?

3. What is the theory for the cause of death?

SECOND DAY

4. The suits are non-_____, so that things can't get through.

5. Why is the helicopter dropping gas?

6. What does the doctor notice about the cuts and bites?

7. Where does blood settle in a normal dead person?

8. What has happened to the blood?

9. How do the doctors find the first survivor?

10. What is the Wildfire research lab disguised as?

11. What is the purpose of the "Key Man"?

12. What material are the suits made out of?

13. What did the Xenon lamp do to the skin?

THIRD DAY

14. The cafeteria has no real food, because it could grow _____

15. What are the three stages of procedure the scientists plan to follow?

     1. _____(determine presence of organism)

     2. _____(structure)

     3. _____(contain)

16. What do the scientists use to determine if the disease is still present in the satellite?

17. _____ study is how a disease enters a body.

18. Why does the door lock behind a person in a special suit when he enters a room with infection?

19. The diameter of the organism is about 2 microns, big enough to be a complete _____

20. What do the scientists find on the rock inside the capsule?

21. What is happening to the pilot's mask?

22. According to the mass spectrometer the "rock" is made of Hydrogen, Carbon, Oxygen, Sulfur, and Silicon, making it very similar to _____.

23. The "Green Stuff" is made of Hydrogen, Carbon, Oxygen, and Nitrogen, which are the _____ on Earth.

24. What are the results of the Amino Acid analysis?

FOURTH DAY
25. What kind of thing is Andromeda?

26. What can Andromeda live on?

27. When the doctors are watching Andromeda on the screen what is it doing?

28. What is wrong with the female doctor?

29. Within what limits can Andromeda live?

30. What has Andromeda mutated into?

31. What is used to protect the central core from escaped animals?

32. What is the Air Force doing to the clouds to kill Andromeda?

Andromeda Strain: Vocabulary

1. Acid   2. Andromeda   3. Bacteria   4. Crystal   5. Disease
6. Epilepsy   7. Infection   8. Laser   9. Mutate   10. Organism
11. pH   12. Porous   13. Respiratory   14. Vacuum   15. Xenon

Andromeda Strain: Discussion questions

1. Triangulation: the process of finding something by knowing its direction from two different places. Using this map of Piedmont, find the missing satellite. Your tracking vans (A & B) have given you the following information. The satellite is south east of van A but it is directly east of van B. Which of the ten houses has the satellite?

Piedmont

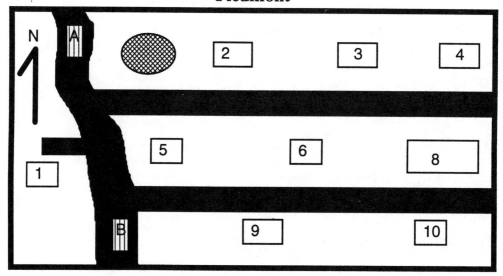

2. What do you think should be the criteria for the "key man"?

3. Why did the people need to be disinfected to be able to proceed to the lower levels?

4. Why were mammals, and not other kinds of animals, used to test the air?

5. Do you think it is reasonable to use animals to test for diseases?

6. Do you think it would be reasonable to use nuclear weapons to stop a disease from spreading?

(explain)

7. For each of the steps of the Scientific Method list a part of the movie that was applicable:

    1. Stating a Problem:

    2. Gathering Information

    3. Suggesting an Answer (hypothesis)

    4. Performing an experiment

    5. Recording and Analyzing Results

    6. Stating Conclusions

8. Look up and state the law of conservation of mass/energy.

Andromeda Strain: Answers to video questions

1. Scoop, the satellite
2. bodies on the ground
3. Scoop satellite
4. porous
5. to kill the birds, to keep them from spreading disease
6. no blood
7. the lowest regions
8. turned solid
9. they hear the crying
10. a research farm
11. to stop the atomic bomb, if needed
12. paper
13. burn off the outer layers
14. bacteria
15. 1) detection, 2)characterization, 3) control
16. a rat and a monkey
17. vector
18. the door locks behind him to keep from spreading disease
19. cell
20. green stuff (life)
21. dissolving (breaking down), turning to powder
22. plastic
23. four basic elements of life on Earth
24. no amino acids
25. a crystal
26. anything
27. dividing and mutating
28. epilepsy/seizure
29. Narrow pH range (near7.3)
30. a non infectious form
31. lasers and gas
32. seeding the clouds

Andromeda Strain: Suggested discussion question answers

1. House #9
2. Answers will vary.
3. Each level down was more "clean" than the level above.
4. The scientist wanted to know how the air would effect humans and were therefore using the most similar animals available.
5. Answers will vary.
6. Answers will vary.
7. Answers will vary (some examples)
    7-1. Something is killing people.
    7-2. Survivors are examined
    7-3. A disease from the satellite is responsible for the deaths.
    7-4. Trying to grow Andromeda in different media.
    7-5. Comparison of blood conditions of survivors to nonsurvivors.
    7-6. Andromeda only survives in a narrow pH range.
8. Matter and Energy can neither be created nor destroyed, they can only change form.

Star Trek®: ARENA
Teacher Information

Content Areas:
Mineral characteristics, chemical reactions, gunpowder.

Synopsis:
While responding to an attack of a Federation outpost, Kirk is kidnapped and placed in a duel. In the process of the duel he finds materials to create gunpowder and construct a crude cannon, which he uses to overcome his opponent.

Good Science:
Video contains accurate descriptions of the properties of the mentioned rocks and minerals. Correct formula for mixing of gunpowder.

Bad Science:
There is no known way for a matter transporter system to work.
There is no known way to travel or communicate faster than light.

Other Information:
Formula for gunpowder: Saltpeter (for nitrates) 75%, charcoal 15%, sulphur 10%

Star Trek®: ARENA

Episode 19   Airdate January 19, 1967
Color   51 minutes
*Better living with Chemistry, or what to do if you ever get kidnapped by super beings and made
        to compete with reptiles.*

Questions to be answered during the video:

1. The Commodore wanted all the _____ crew from the ship to come down to the planet's surface.

2. Kirk's evaluation is that Cescus 3 has been _____.

3. What is the survivor found by the landing party suffering from?

4. What reason does Spock give that the lifeforms he is reading are not survivors?

5. Why can't Kirk and the rest of the crew be "beamed" back to the ship?

6. Back onboard the ship, what does the injured man say the aliens did?

7. What does Kirk believe that the attack was the start of?

8. The Enterprise is being "scanned" from _____

9. What is the Phaser Bank report after the ship has been stopped?

10. Who stopped the ship?

11. What have the Metrons set up to occur between captains?

12. What is the reptile being called?

13. How does Kirk escape the lizard captain's hold?

14. As Kirk surveys the land he says that there are scrub brush, rocks and an abundance of

    _____

15. Diamonds are the _____ substance known to man.

16. What is the yellow mineral on the ground?

17. What does Spock think is the white substance on the rock?

18. What reason does the reptile captain give for the attack?

19. What else does Spock say that Kirk needs to find?

20. What chemical mixture is Kirk making?

21. Describe the appearance of coal:

22. What has Kirk made?

23. What purpose does the rope serve?

24. How old is the Metrone?

25. What behavior did Captain Kirk show that impressed the Metrones?

Arena: Vocabulary

1. Combustion   2. Compound   3. Element
4. Mineral   5. Parsec   6. Predator
7. Radiation   8. Reptile   9. Species
10. Tactical

Arena: Discussion questions

1. Who do you think was more right and why? (Earthling or Gorn)

2. Can you think of an American History example of such a conflict starting?

3. Do you think that problems between nations should be solved by the leaders fighting?

4. What is the chemical symbol for sulfur and the formula for potassium nitrate?

5. Diamonds and coal are both made of the same element. What is that element and its symbol?

6. Do you think that the cannon would have worked and why?

Arena: Answers to video questions

1. tactical
2. destroyed
3. radiation burns, shock, internal injury
4. cold-blooded
5. defensive screens up
6. attacked without warning
7. invasion
8. a solar system
9. inoperable, no power
10. Metrons
11. contest
12. Gorn
13. hits the Gorn in the ears (boxes)
14. minerals
15. hardest
16. sulfur
17. potassium nitrate
18. federation invaded their space
19. charcoal or coal
20. gunpowder
21. black, rock like
22. cannon
23. keep from exploding out
24. 1500
25. mercy

Arena: Suggested discussion answers
1. Answers will vary.
2. European countries colonizing North America. Answers will vary.
3. Answers will vary.
4. The symbol for sulfur is S and the formula for potassium nitrate is KNO_3.
5. They both are made of carbon (C).
6. Answers will vary.

Star Trek the Next Generation®: HOME SOIL
Teacher Information

Content Areas:
Hydrogeology, requirements for life, scientific method, organic & inorganic chemistry.

Synopsis:
The crew of the Enterprise visits a planet that is in the process of terraforming, when an engineer is killed under strange circumstances. An inorganic, intelligent lifeform is discovered and studied using the scientific method. A struggle ensues for control of the Enterprise between the crew and the crystal lifeform. The crew finally wins by turning out the lights.

Good Science:
An excellent example of using a scientific approach to problem solving.
A discussion of the requirements for determining what is life.
The properties of the chemicals discussed.

Bad Science:
There is no known way for a matter transporter system to work.
There is no known way to travel or communicate faster than light.

Star Trek the Next Generation®: HOME SOIL

Episode 17   Air Date 2/22/88
Color   46 Minutes
"A question of what is life?"

Questions to be answered during the video:

1. What is the base on Velara 3 doing to the planet?

2. What does Troi sense that director Mandel is doing?

3. What is Data?

4. Terraforming changes a lifeless planet into one that can _____

5. What compound is involved in phase 3?

6. After there is water on the planet, what is introduced next?

7. The water table is sandwiched between layers of sand and rock thereby maintaining a

   constant _____.

8. What killed the hydrologic engineer?

9. What does Data do to the laser drill?

10. What does Geordi see down the drill tunnel?

11. What reason does Geordi give for saying it is not alive?

12. These are the basic requirements for _____.
assimilate	respirate	reproduce	grow
develop	move	secrete	excrete

13. List one of the steps of the scientific method.

14. The computer says the sample is not organic because it lacks what element?

15. What happens to the "humming" as the people step back?

16. What behavior is the sample exhibiting that makes the computer think it is life?

17. How do the people know the sample is about to change?

18. Why does Data say that the sample is alive?

19. How does the Captain know that it is an intelligent life form?

20. How did the terraformers first become aware of the local lifeform?

21-23 Match:

21. Silicon and Germanium are _____ materials   a. conductor

22. Gallium and Arsenide emit _____ when charged.   b. transistor

23. Cadmium Siliconide Sulfide emit ___ when lit.   c. light

24. Water and Sodium salts act as _____.   d. charge

25. How does the lifeform call/describe people?

26. Who actually killed Mallison (hydraulic engineer)?

27. What does the Captain now call the lifeform?

28. With single cell lifeforms, reproduction is preceded by a _____.

29. Why is the saline layer on the planet important to the Microbrains?

30. How does the Captain try to stop the Mircobrain.

31. For how long does the Microbrain send people away?

Home Soil: Vocabulary

1. Android	8. Excrete	15. Organic
2. Arable	9. Factor	16. Phase
3. Carbon	10. Hydraulic	17. Photoelectric
4. Conductor (elect.)	11. Inorganic	18. Quarantine
5. Dormant	12. Laser	19. Saline
6. Dynamic	13. Life	20. Secrete
7. Evacuate	14. Microorganism	21. Watertable

Home Soil: Discussion questions

1. What conditions are necessary for the microbrains on Velara III?

2. Give an example of something humans do for each of the mentioned requirements of life:

     a. Assimilate: b. Reproduce

     c. Respirate   d. Grow

     e. Develop   f. Move

     g. Secrete   h. Excrete

3. How is the Microbrain similar to a computer?

4. a. Name three living things:

  b. Name three nonliving things:

  c. Can you think of something with characteristics of both living and nonliving things?

5. Why did the Microbrain send people away for 300 years?

6. In observing the microbrain at first, why did the people have difficulty recognizing that it was

     a lifeform?

Home Soil: Answers to video questions
1. terraforming
2. that he is concealing something
3. android
4. support life
5. water
6. microorganisms
7. depth
8. laser drill
9. destroys it
10. basic elements, no carbon, light flashes
11. inorganic
12. organic life
13. observe, theory, attempt to prove (experiment)
14. carbon
15. goes down
16. nonpattern flashes
17. Geordi sees a change in the infrared
18. it reproduces
19. it is trying to communicate
20. patterns in the sand
21. transistor
22. light
23. charge
24. conductor
25. ugly giant bags of mostly water
26. crystal lifeform
27. microbrain
28. resting state
29. connect/connective tissue
30. turn off the lights
31. 300 years

Home Soil: Suggested discussion answers
1. A specific temperature, light, and salinity level.
2.   a. Eat   b. Have children   c. Breathe   d. Get taller
        e. Grow up   f. Walk   h. Sweat   h. Go to the bathroom

3. Composed of inorganic materials using electricity. Answers will vary.
4. a. b. c. Answers will vary.
5. To give them time as a race to mature.
6. Composed of inorganic materials, and did not resemble any familiar living things.

95

Conductivity Tester

Construct a conductivity indicator instrument using inexpensive materials *(available from Radio Shack or other electronics suppliers).*

Materials:
9-Volt battery
Insulated wire (such as speaker wire)
9-Volt battery replacement snap *(Radio Shack Cat. No. 270-350)*
Blinking red LED *(Cat. No. 276-036B)*
1k ohm resistor *(Cat. No. 271-1321)*
Electrical tape
Pencil leads
Non-conductive rod (e.g. an old ballpoint pen body)

Construction:
The conductivity tester is assembled according to the diagram as shown and described below. All bare wire (except electrodes) should be covered with electrical tape. The 1k resistor is connected to the black wire of the battery cap, the negative side (short wire) of the LED is connected to the resistor, and the positive end of the LED goes to an electrode. The red wire from the battery cap goes to the other electrode. Electrodes can be made out of copper wire or mechanical pencil leads. The whole setup can be taped onto an old plastic ballpoint pen for easy use.

Procedure:
Immerse the electrodes into solutions that are to be tested. The blinking style of the LED shows the nature of the solution's conductivity:
Blinking = strong conductor;
dull red glow = weak conductor;
no glow or no blink = poor conductor or non-conductor.
Electrodes should be rinsed in distilled water before each test.

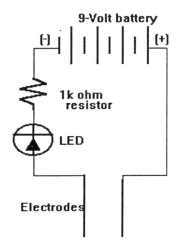

SCHEMATIC DIAGRAM

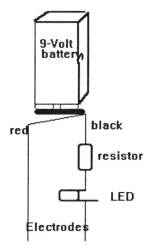

GENERAL DIAGRAM

Data Table					
Liquid	LED	Conductivity	Liquid	LED	Conductivity

pH & Indicators

pH is a measure of the strength of an acid or base. pH ranges on its scale from 0 to 14. Any pH less than 7 is an acid, greater than 7 a base. If the pH is 7 then the solution is neutral. Look up the pH values of five different common substances. pH can be determined using indicators. An indicator is a substance that changes (usually color) when its surroundings change.

Materials:
Rubbing Alcohol
White Paper
 (coffee filters work well)
Turmeric Spice
X-Lax containing
    phenolphthalein
Small Bowls
Ammonia
Hand Soap (bar)
Vinegar
Flowers (bright color)
Heat source
Pot or pan with water

In this lab you will make three different indicators.:

1. Turmeric Indicator: Put about a teaspoon of turmeric spice with two tablespoons of rubbing alcohol. Now dip some white paper (coffee filters work great) into the mixture. The paper should turn bright yellow. Let the paper dry. Turmeric will turn red-brown in the presence of a strong base (such as household ammonia or soap) and yellow in the presence of an acid (such as vinegar).

2. Phenolphthalein Indicator: Using some Ex-Lax with phenol, dissolve one of the pills in about 5 tablespoons of rubbing alcohol. Adding a base will cause this indicator to turn pink and adding an acid will cause this indicator to turn clear. (It works great as secret message paint, just spray with weak ammonia or rub with soap)

3. Flower Indicator: Gather some brightly colored flowers (reds work well). Rip up the petals and boil them in a small amount of water. Boil the petals for about 5 minutes. Observe the color formed. Pour some of the water from the flower liquid into a cup. Add some acid to the solution and look for a color change. Rinse out the cup. Try the experiment again but using a base to look for a color change.

	Data Table					
Indicator:	Turmeric		Phenolphthalein		Flower	
Solution	Acid	Base	Acid	Base	Acid	Base
Color						

Observations:

Crystal Growth

Crystals are any solid that is made up of particles that are arranged in regular, repeating patterns. Every crystal, of the same type, no matter what size, has the same geometric shape. Crystals have some important properties, one of which is that they can grow.

Materials:
Laundry Blueing
Ammonia
Water
Salt
Small Bowl
Coffee Filter
Magnifying Lens
Optional:
Food coloring
Charcoal

In this lab you will grow some crystals from a liquid solution.
1. Make a solution using a mixture of salt, ammonia, and laundry blueing.
2. Mix together 6 tablespoons of laundry blueing, 1 tablespoon of ammonia, 6 tablespoons of water, and 6 tablespoons of table salt.
3. Pour the liquid solution into a shallow dish.
4. Put a coffee filter that has been shaped into a tee-pee (or a lump of charcoal) into the dish (filter acts as a wick). If you put food coloring onto the coffee filter (or the charcoal) the crystals will grow that color.
5. Wait several hours and observe (use a magnifying lens). This growth process is slow as the crystals will form as evaporation occurs. .
6. Leave the setup out over the next few days, and carefully add more solution if needed.
Caution: the crystals grown are very delicate and fragile.

Observations:

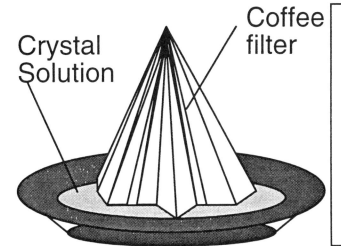
Crystal Solution

Coffee filter

Crystal Diagram

Earth Science:

Crack in the World
Earthquake
Journey to the Center of the Earth

Activities:
Locate an Earthquake Epicenter,
Flame Tests

CRACK IN THE WORLD
Teacher Information

Content Areas:
Geology, plate tectonics, earth interior, vulcanism, earthquakes, nuclear explosions, natural satellites

Synopsis:
Scientists trying to tap into a new source of power drill through the Earth's crust to reach the magma. When they are stopped by a super hard layer, they use a nuclear bomb to break through, accidently triggering a series of earthquakes. The earthquakes, following fault lines, break through the crust, and cause a section of the Earth's crust to be blown into space forming a new moon.

Good Science:
Increasing temperature with depth.
Fault and trench structures and their relationships.
Instrumentation (seismographs, spectrographs)
Geothermal energy
Movie does follow the daughter theory of moon formation.
Contains lots of good volcano film.

Bad Science:
Daughter theory is not caused by a steam explosion.
Earth's cross-section diagram is out of proportion.
Volcanos are a major source of pollution.

Other:
As of this book being published, Crack in the World is not yet available on videotape, but is frequently shown on the American Movie Classics cable channel.

CRACK IN THE WORLD

Directed by Andrew Marton *First shown 1965*
Color *96 minutes*
Drilling through the Earth's crust for power, or beyond the Moho.

Questions to be answered during the video:

1. In what continent is the project based?

2. Goupolle is in charge of what instrument?

3. To help combat Dr. Sorenson's rash on his hand he is receives a large dose of _____.

4. What is the target that the project is trying to reach?

5. In the Ransian theory, what kind of blast runs the risk of breaking the Earth?

6. The project goal to make _____.

7. Who gives the "go ahead"?

8. What does the doctor tell Steven Sorenson about his disease?

9. From what area is Dr. Ransian's sounding evidence taken?

10. What happens after the rocket is fired?

11. Name one of the metals found in "magma":

12. What is the heat going to be used to generate?

13. Why were the animals scared?

14. After the Port Victoria disaster, what happened to the island other than violent tremors?

15. What was found using the mini submarine?

16. The experiment has caused a crack in the earth's _____.

17. What is the volcanic eruption line moving along?

18. What type of "graph" is being used to analyze the atomic explosions?

19. What element was found in the project's experiment that was not in the previous atomic explosions?

20. What are they going to use a nuclear bomb to relieve?

21. To what temperature have the protective suits been tested?

22. What happens to Steel?

23. Why does Ransian collapse?

24. For what purpose are the protective filters used?

25. After the volcano island explodes, what happens to the crack?

26. What is happening to the seismograph signals at the project?

27. Where do the cracks seem to be converging?

28. What does Dr. Sorenson think will happen to 20,000 square miles of the Earth's crust?

29. What happens to the train?

30. Sorenson staying to record the birth of what?

Crack in the World: Vocabulary
1. Core   2. Crust   3. Fault
4. Geologist   5. Magma   6. Seismograph
7. Sounding   8. Spectrograph   9. Theory
10. Trench   11. Tsunami (tidal wave)   12. Volcano

Crack in the World: Discussion questions
1. Look up in your science book, or a reference book, a cross section of the Earth and label the
       parts. What section was missing from the video?

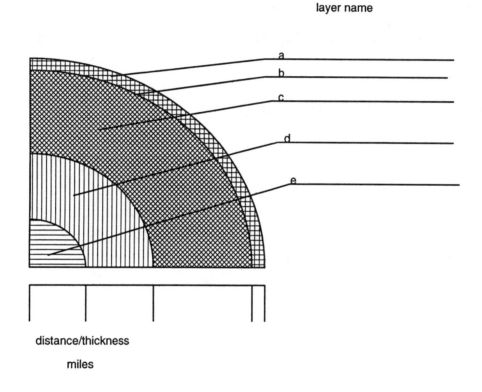

2. Would bringing magma to the surface of the Earth for a power source actually be clean and
       nonpolluting?

3. Cracks in the world actually exist in area of seafloor spreading called mid-ocean ridges. Make
       a map of the world and add these ridges onto the map.

4. Would you stand on the beach and watch if the next island over was blown up by nuclear and
       volcanic explosions? Why or Why Not?

5. Considering that the escape velocity of an object from the Earth is about 7 miles per second, is it reasonable to think that the people could escape harm by running away (like at the end of the movie)?

6. In a science or reference book look up the current theories about the formation of our moon. Does the movie come close to any of those theories?

7. Dr. Sorenson states (factually) that at the depth of the lab, the temperature would be over 200° Fahrenheit, because for every 60 feet below the surface you go, the temperature goes up 1 degree Fahrenheit. The actual thickness of the crust is only a few miles (2 miles under oceans to 20 miles under continents). Calculate the temperature for depth on a graph or for some specific distances (remember 5280 feet = 1 mile).

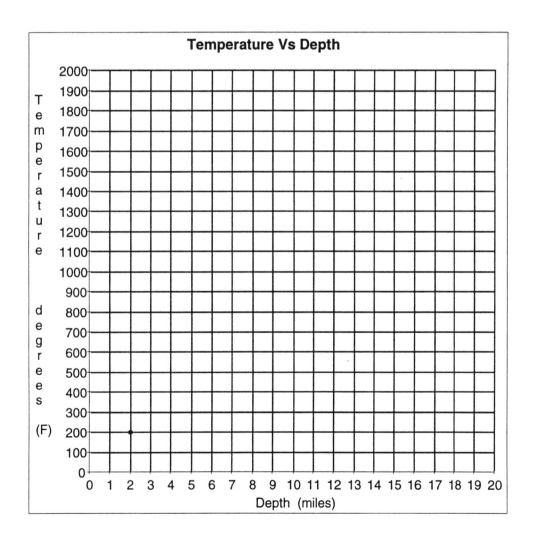

Crack in the World: Answers to video questions

1. Africa
2. seismographs
3. X-rays
4. magma/core
5. nuclear/atomic
6. clean power
7. the committee
8. can't be stopped, malignant
9. soundings of the fault area
10. area explodes and "volcano" is formed
11. nickel, molybdenum, iron
12. electricity
13. tremors, earthquake
14. tidal wave
15. underwater volcanos/they have opened a deep fissure in ocean floor.
16. crust
17. fault line
18. spectrograph
19. Hydrogen
20. pressure
21. 1000 degrees
22. breaks his cable and falls into the volcano
23. heat/poison gas
24. brightness of the explosion
25. moving twice as fast and in a new direction
26. getting weaker
27. at the project bore hole
28. thrown (blown) into space
29. falls into the crack
30. a moon

Crack in the World: Suggested discussion answers

1.

a. Crust	b. Moho	c. Mantle	d. Outer Core	e. Inner Core
3-56 mi	0	(3-56)-1800 mi	1800-3762 mi	3762-3958 mi

The relative thicknesses of the layers were wrong in the movie's diagram.
2. Yes it could be clean, but volcanos do emit some pollutant gases.
3. Mid-ocean ridges are located in the Atlantic, Pacific, and Indian oceans.
4. No, fallout and shock wave would kill you.
5. No the amout of mass moved during the explosion would trigger very large earthquakes and disruptions.
6. Yes, very similar to the sister & daughter theories of moon formation.
7. Temp = (Depth in miles) * (88 °F/mi)

EARTHQUAKE
Teacher Information

Content Areas:
Earthquakes, seismology, emergency management, and natural disasters.

Synopsis:
An earthquake devastates Los Angeles. In the film, data collected and other occurrences observed seem to lead to the prediction of an earthquake. The earthquake occurs and the story continues with the efforts of people to survive after a major earthquake.

Good Science:
Earthquake scales and measurements.
Instrumentation.
Fault activity.
Realistic dangers from earthquakes, and their aftereffects.

Bad Science:
At the motorcycle race track, the speeds that the cyclist uses are too slow for the stunts.
The apparent length of time the quake lasted was too long.

EARTHQUAKE

Directed by Mark Robson   First Shown 1974
Color   123 minutes   Rated PG

Questions to be answered during the video:

1. In what city does the earthquake take place?

2. What did the two men have to do to the dam after the earthquake?

3. What was the strength of the first earthquake?

4. What scale is used to measure earthquakes?

5. On what instrument at the seismological institute are earthquakes measured?

6. How big does Russell predict the next big earthquake will be, and when?

7. What geological feature was Adams on when he died?

8. What did the governor put on active duty status?

9. How does Mrs. Brian know something is about to happen?

10. What was wrong with the man who went to turn off the gas?

11. Why did the men want to open the valves on the dam?

12. What are some of the dangers after an earthquake?

13. What is the military doing when they are put on the streets?

14. What are they worried about happening at the dam, after the earthquake that might cause the dam to collapse?

15. Where do the police check for blood?

16. Why do the escalators work in the shelter?

17. How do they know that there is trouble with the dam, after the aftershocks but before the leaks?

Earthquake: Vocabulary

1. Aftershock
3. Fault
5. Predict
7. Seismic
9. Shelter

2. Earthquake
4. Generator
6. Richter Scale
8. Seismograph
10. Wave

Earthquake: Discussion questions:

1. According to the film, what places are safe during an earthquake?

2. Where is a very unsafe place to be during a quake?

3. Do you think that this movie is an accurate portrayal of what would happen during an earthquake?

4. What do you think cities should do to plan for earthquakes?

5. If you lived in an earthquake zone, you should make an earthquake emergency bag. What do you think should be stored in that bag, considering that all water and power will be off for at least the next three days after an earthquake?

6. Match the following to the diagram:

   1. epicenter   2. fault   3. focus   4. seismic wave

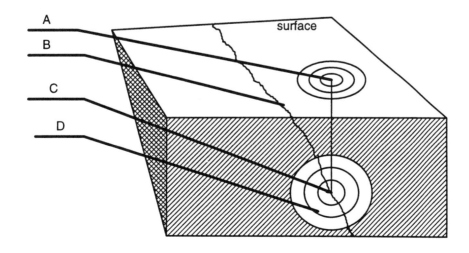

Earthquake: Answers to video questions
1. LA, Hollywood
2. emergency inspection
3. 3.1
4. Richter scale
5. seismograph
6. 7+
7. fault
8. National Guard
9. dogs barking and howling
10. he was smoking
11. relieve the pressure behind the dam
12. fire, flood, electrical wires, looting
13. stopping looters
14. aftershocks
15. Red Cross
16. building has its own generator
17. door is out of line

Earthquake: Suggested discussion answers
1. Underneath strong supported objects (like arches or cars)
2. Outside of large glass structures, buildings with poor support, answers will vary.
3. Answers will vary (but the usual length of an earthquake occurance is less than a minute)
4. Storage of emgergency materials such as food, water, blankets, machinery, medicine, and communication equipment. Answers will vary.
5. Answers will vary.
6. A-1 B-2   C-3   D-4   E-5

JOURNEY TO THE CENTER OF THE EARTH
Teacher Information

Content Areas:
Volcanism, Earth's interior, caves, rocks and minerals.

Synopsis:
A group of explorers enters a volcano to follow the path of a previous explorer, to the center of the Earth. They encounter cave formations, lost civilizations, dinosaurs, mineral deposits, and the great underground ocean. The explorers are able to escape from the center of the Earth using a volcanic chimney to the surface.

Good Science:
There are caves formed by volcanos
There are forms of luminescent algae.
Mushrooms do grow underground.
The temperature does rise as you go underground.

Bad Science:
The caves shown in the movie are solution caves, not volcanic cave formations.
Magnets don't attract gold.
Really bad dinosaur depiction. (lizards with collars)
The great underground ocean.
The amount of light present.
The depth to which the caves extended and connected. (center of the Earth is liquid metal)

JOURNEY TO THE CENTER OF THE EARTH

Directed by Henry Levin *First shown 1959*
Color   129 minutes
Based on the book by Jules Verne

Questions to be answered during the video:

1. What year does the film start?

2. Professor Lendenbrook is a professor of _____.

3. What kind of rock (made out of what) is given to the professor by the student?

4. What is the professor trying to do to the rock?

5. What was found inside the rock?

6. Where was Sorenson trying to go when he died?

7. On what island country was the volcano that Sorenson entered?

8. On what day does the mountain point the way to the entrance?

9. What is Gertrude?

10. What is special about the lights that they will be using?

11. What compound killed Professor Gurturbourg?

12. Who was the last person to see Professor Gurturbourg?

13. What is Mrs. Gurturbourg's condition about letting Lendenbrook have the equipment?

14. How does the mountain show the gateway (cave entrance)?

15. Why can't the expedition go down the hole?

16. Why can the people use their canteens freely now?

17. What is the sign that Arne Sorenson used?

18. How does Count Sorenson fool the expedition?

19. What formations continued on the 21st day?

20. What is found in the hole into which Alec fell?

21. Why does the woman have to remove her corset (stays)?

22. Why does the wall collapse?

23. What is the white material that Alec finds?

24. Of what did the servant die?

25. How does the professor get the gun from the Count?

26. What is cooler than expected?

27. What causes the light?

28. In what kind of mineral deposit is the expedition on Day 256?

29. What does Alec find to eat?

30. The dimetradon is a _____ eater.

31. What metal is attracted at the junction of the magnetic poles?

32. What happened to Gertrude?

33. What lost city is found?

34. Of what fireproof material is the large alter bowl made?

35. A volcanic _____ with an updraft is the way out.

36. What will they use to remove the rock blocking the passage?

37. What does the explosion start?

38. How does the expedition escape the center of the Earth?

39. What did Alec lose?

40. "If a scientist can't _____ his accomplishments then he has

accomplished nothing."

Journey to the Center of the Earth: Vocabulary

1. Cinnabar	2. Core	3. Crust
4. Density	5. Expedition	6. Lava
7. Limestone	8. Magma	9. Mantle
10. Stalagmite	11. Stalactite	12. Volcano

Journey to the Center of the Earth: Discussion questions

1. In the video the Professor states that the Lava Rock is too dense to have come from a Mediterranean volcano. Do lava rocks come in different densities?

2. What problems do you see with four people carrying their supplies for a prolonged expedition under the earth?

3. Since the temperature goes up 1 degree Fahrenheit for every 20 meters down below the Earth's surface, what would have been the temperature rise when the expedition was twenty kilometers (20,000 meters) beneath the surface?

4. The requirements for mushroom growth are dark, damp, fertile areas. What kind of living things are mushrooms? How well do you think mushrooms could grow underground?

5. If the dimetrodons are carnivores, what could their food source have been for them to survive?

6. In the movie it was said that a luminescent algae was making the light. Name a plant or animal that can make light.

7. What kind of metal do magnets actually attract? (no magnet attracts gold)

8. Label the following cave parts
   a. columns   b. shelf   c. stalactites   d. stalagmites

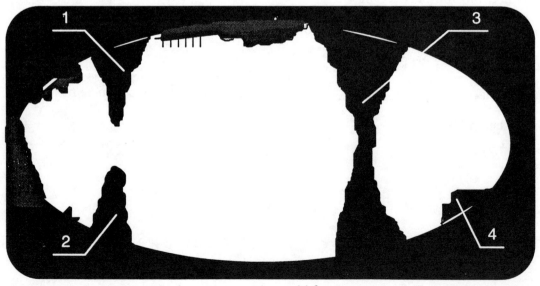

Journey to the Center of the Earth: Answers to video questions

1. 1880
2. geology
3. lava
4. melt off the outside
5. a plumb bob
6. to the center of the Earth
7. Iceland
8. sunrise on the last day of May.
9. a duck/goose
10. Bruencorff lamps, self generated
11. potassium cyanide
12. Count Sorenson
13. that she gets to go along
14. sunlight shines through a hole in the mountain
15. too deep
16. there are lots of mineral springs near he surface
17. three notches cut into the rock
18. cuts new notches and covers up the old ones
19. limestone formations
20. water and crystals
21. they are going into an area where it will be hot
22. breaks under water pressure when a crystal specimen is taken
23. salt
24. too much heat, load, and fear
25. throws salt in his face (eyes)
26. the air temperature
27. a form of algae, chemoluminscence
28. cinnabar
29. mushrooms
30. flesh
31. gold
32. she was eaten by the Count
33. Atlantis
34. asbestos
35. chimney
36. gunpowder
37. a volcanic eruption
38. rides up in a bowl inside a volcano to the surface
39. his pants
40. prove

Journey to the Center of the Earth: Suggested discussion answers

1. Yes, depending on composition and formation.
2. Answers will vary.
3. 1000°F
4. Mushrooms are Fungi, and they grow very well underground as long as their needs are met (they don't need sunlight).
5. Other animals.
6. Some types of insects (Fireflies), some types of algae, some type of jellies (jelly fish), some type of fish and sea fireflies.
7. Iron based.
8. 1-c 2-d 3-1 4-b

Locate an Earthquake Epicenter

When an earthquake occurs seismic waves are sent out in all directions. Earthquake waves come in three main types: P-waves (primary); S-waves (secondary); and L-waves (surface). These waves travel at different speeds:
P-waves being fastest, S-waves being next fastest, and L-waves the slowest. By knowing the time difference between when any two types of earthquake waves arrive at any particular place you can deduce how far away the earthquake epicenter is. By contacting other seismographic stations it is possible to determine where the earthquake occured.

In this activity you will use seismographic data and a compass to find the epicenter of an earthquake.

Procedure:
1. Calculate the time difference for when the waves were received at each station.
2. Use the Graph to find the distance from the station to the epicenter.
3. Using the scale on the map, draw a circle around each station, with a radius of the circle equal to that station's distance from the epicenter.
4. Mark the point of intersection for all circles: this is where the earthquake occurred.

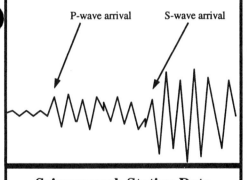

Seismograph Station Data

Station A:
   P-wave arrival: 10:05 AM
   S-wave arrival: 10:08 AM

Station B:
   P-wave arrival: 10:10 AM
   S-wave arrival: 10:14:30 AM

Station C:
   P-wave arrival: 10:13 AM
   S-wave arrival: 10:20 AM

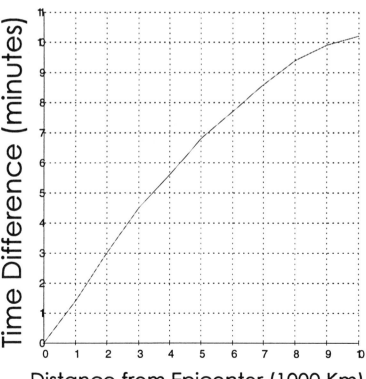

Earthquake Waves & Distance

Time Difference (minutes)

Distance from Epicenter (1000 Km)

119

Locate an Epicenter Map

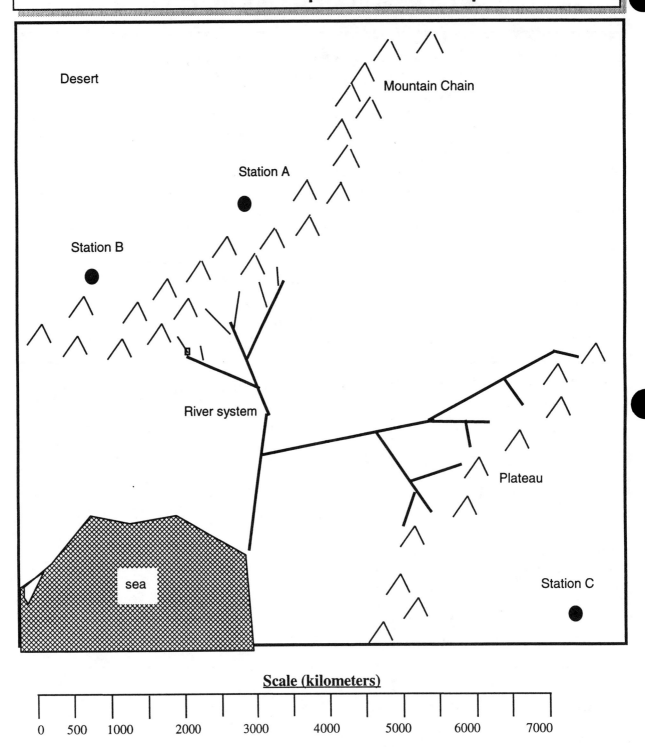

Scale (kilometers)

| 0 | 500 | 1000 | 2000 | 3000 | 4000 | 5000 | 6000 | 7000 |

Flame Tests

Just as a fingerprint is unique to each person, the color of light emitted after excitation of an element is different for each element. When a metallic element's electrons absorb energy, by heating for example, the electron is said to become "excited". When an excited electron moves back to its "ground state" (non-excited), energy is emitted in the form of light.

Materials:
Toothpicks or wood splints
Paper cups
Large candle
Metal pie pan
Distilled water
Pliers or tongs

Solutions made from metal compounds:
  Calcium (calcium chloride)
  Copper (copper chloride)
  Potassium (potassium chloride)
  Sodium (sodium chloride)

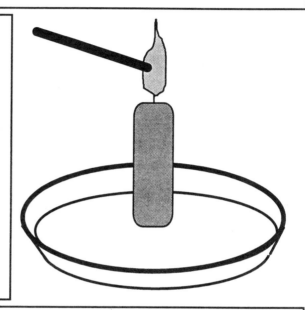

Procedure:
1. Dissolve a small amount of each metal compound in distilled water. (The concentration is not important) Use a separate paper cup for each metal solution. Label the cups with the names of the metal solutions. Fill and label one cup with plain distilled water to serve as a control.
2. Soak some wood splints or toothpicks in each solution cup.
3. Place a candle securely in the metal pie pan, and pour some water in the pan. Light the candle, remembering flame safety.
4. Use the tongs or pliers to hold a toothpick so the soaked end is in the candle's flame. Observe the color, and record data in the table below.

Data Table			
Metal	**Color**	**Metal**	**Color**
Calcium		Potassium	
Copper		Sodium	

Environmental Science/Ecology:

StarTrek IV
Trouble with Tribbles

Activity:
Qualitative Testing of Carbon
Dioxide; a Pollutant

StarTrek® IV: THE VOYAGE HOME
Teacher Information

Content Areas:
Whale biology, endangered species, environmental chemistry, global warming, communication, hydrodynamics, and material science.

Synopsis:
An unknown probe heading to the Earth attempts to communicate with a now extinct species. As a side effect of the attempt at communication, the probe is causing destruction. In order to get a whale for communication with the probe, Kirk and his crew travel back in time to collect a whale.

Good Science:
The film accurately portrays the current conditions and behaviors of humpback whales. Whales are tracked using radio transmitters.
It is possible to determine the year by comparison of the atmosphere composition (i.e. carbon dioxide level).

Bad Science:
There is no known way for a matter transporter system to work.
There is no known way to travel or communicate faster than light.
Aluminum has no known transparent form.

Other:
Caution: teachers should preview this film to make sure the language is appropriate.
Contact your local science education specialist or research other sources about the Inland Whale Project. The Inland Whale Project has plans that allow students to construct their own life-size inflatable whale.

StarTrek® IV: THE VOYAGE HOME

Directed by Leonard Nimoy   *First Shown 1986*
Color   119 minutes
Whales save the world!

Questions to be answered during the video:

1. What do the Klingons want?

2. What does Dr. McCoy name the new ship?

3. What does the unknown probe do the space ship Saratoga?

4. To what planet is the probe on a direct path?

5. The space station/space dock has lost all internal _____.

6. What seemed to happen to the ocean after the station lost power?

7. By how much has the cloud cover increased?

8. What part of the Earth does the probe ionize?

9. For what does Kirk have the communications officer modify the probe signal?

10. What is the probe transmission?

11. When during the film did whales become extinct?

12. What is the weight of an adult humpback?

13. Where on Earth will Kirk look for whales?

14. What object in solar system does the ship use to increase speed?

15. What does Spock use to determine the current date?

16. In what city does the ship land?

17. At what institute are the whales?

18. Whales are what kind of animals?

19. Most whales don't have _____, instead they have baleen.

20. What species is the whales' principal enemy?

21. Today there are less than _____ humpback whales?

22. How much food can whales eat per day?

23. Which of the whales will sing?

24. What will happen when the whales are released?

25. What has happened to the whale Gracie?

26. How thick would the plexi-glass need to be to withstand the high pressure?

27. How are the whales tagged?

28. What happened to the whales?

29. To where have the whales have been shipped?

30. What is the radio frequency of the whales' transmitters?

31. What kind of ship is closing on the whales?

32. What do whaling ships use to kill whales?

33. "They say the sea is cold but that the sea contains the hottest blood of all" is from a poem by T.H. Lawrence. What is the name of the poem?

34. What will happen to the whales if they stay stuck inside the sinking ship?

35. How do the whales save the Earth?

36. What is Kirk's new ship?

StarTrek IV: Vocabulary
1. Baleen   2. Blowhole   3. Cetacean
4. Extinct   5. Flipper   6. Fluke
7. Ionized   8. Mammal   9. Saline
10. Species

StarTrek IV: Discussion questions
1. Match the following terms to the whale diagram

Blowhole	Dorsal fin	Ear	Eye
Flippers	Flukes	Mouth	

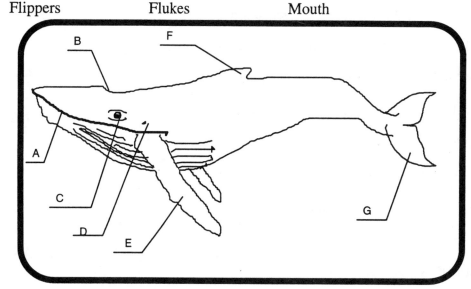

2. How can whales drown?
3. Whales can communicate over 100's of miles with their singing. Why can't we speak for over 100 yards?
4. The whales in the movie were baleen whales, the other kind of whales are called toothed. How do you think toothed whales are different from baleen whales?
5. What could you do to help protect whales?
6. Spock uses pollution as a method of determining the current year. How could this work?
7. What would be the effect of 100% cloud cover all around the world?

Mini Project
8. Break the class down into small groups. Each group will research to do a mini report and make a picture on one of the following types of whales:

BELUGA WHALE	BLUE WHALE
GRAY WHALE	ORCA (KILLER WHALE)
NARWHAL	RIGHT WHALE
SPERM WHALE	RIVER DOLPHIN (AMAZON OR GANGES)
PORPOISE	DOLPHIN

(Yes there is a difference between dolphins and porpoises)

StarTrek IV: Answers to video questions

1. Kirk
2. Bounty
3. cuts out all power
4. Earth
5. power
6. lifted up
7. 78 %
8. the atmosphere
9. depth, temperature and salinity
10. is the song sung by whales (humpback whales)
11. extinct since the 23rd century
12. 40 tons
13. Pacific ocean
14. sun
15. pollution amounts
16. San Francisco
17. Cetacean Institute
18. mammals
19. teeth
20. man
21. 10,000
22. 2 tons of shrimp
23. whale song is sung by the male singing up to 30 min.
24. at risk from whale hunters
25. pregnant
26. 6 inches
27. with radio transmitters
28. they left last night
29. Alaska
30. 401 megahertz
31. whaling ship
32. harpoon
33. "Whales Weep Not"
34. the whales will drown
35. they sing and the probe goes away
36. the Enterprise 1701-A

StarTrek IV: Suggested discussion answers

1. A. Mouth   B. Blowhole   C. Eye   D. Ear   E. Flipper
    F. Dorsal Fin   G. Flukes
2. Since whales breathe air, if they stay too long underwater they can drown. (they can't breathe water)
3. Air is less dense than water, and therefore sound can't travel as well.
4. Toothed whales are usually hunters while baleen whales graze on krill.
5. Answers will vary.
6. Some types of pollution have been studied for a long time, so if you compare the percentage of a pollutant in the atmosphere you can determine the approximate year.
7. Lower the temperature by blocking out sunlight.
8. Answers will vary.

Star Trek®: The Trouble with Tribbles
Teacher Information

Content Areas:
Exotic species, genetic engineering, animal biology.

Synopsis:
A new animal, called a tribble, is being sold at a spacestation. The spacestation is storing grain for use on a planet. The tribbles begin reproducing after being fed and soon the Enterprise and the spacestation are overrun with tribbles. The tribbles get into the grain storage and begin to feed. Most of the tribbles found in the grain are dead. The dead tribbles expose the plot of poisoning the grain.

Good Science:
The effects of moving animals out of their natural habitat can be destructive to the new environment.
New forms of plants (hybrid) are created by genetic engineering.

Bad Science:
There is no known way for a matter transporter system to work.
There is no known way to travel or communicate faster than light.

Other:
A real life example of these extremes of overpopulation of a species in a new environment is what happened when rabbits were introduced to Australia. They overpopulated so quickly because of the lack of natural predators that they soon exhausted their food sources.

Star Trek®:
THE TROUBLE WITH TRIBBLES

Episode 42   Airdate December 29, 1967
  Color   51 minutes
A problem involving exotics.

Questions to be answered during the video:

1. What determines who gets Sherman's planet?

2. What does a "priority one" distress call mean?

3. What is in the space station's storage compartment? (use common name)

4. Describe a tribble's physical features and behaviors.

5. Transporting _____ animals from one planet to another is against regulations.

6. What material did Checkov feed the tribble?

7. What do the Klingons state is their reason for visiting the space station K7?

8. What is the effect of the tribble's sound on humans?

9. How much of the tribble's metabolism is dedicated to reproduction?

10. What happens if tribbles eat too much?

11. What is the tribble's reaction to a Klingon?

12. What kept tribbles from overpopulating their natural habitat?

13. a. How many tribbles are in an average litter?

   b. How often can they reproduce?

14. What keeps tribbles from reproducing?

15. What was the problem with the grain?

Tribbles: Vocabulary

1. Exotic
2. Parsec
3. Hybrid
4. Dissect
5. Metabolism

6. Reproduction
7. Parasite
8. Bisexual
9. Predator
10. Habitat

11. Prolific
12. Virus
13. Inert
14. Litter
15. Poison

Tribbles: Discussion questions

1. What makes an animal harmful?

2. What are the troubles with tribbles?

3. What are some exotics in your environment?

4. What kind of problems can exotics cause?

5. How should "exotic" be defined?

6. Are all exotics harmful?

7. What should be done about exotics?

8. What should have been done about the tribbles on the Enterprise?

9. What kind of organisms can be exotics (other than animals)?

10. What kind of pets are exotics?

Trouble With Tribbles: Answers to video questions
1. who can best use it
2. emergency of the highest order, immediate threat
3. wheat
4. furry, easygoing
5. dangerous
6. wheat
7. rest and relaxation
8. soothing
9. 50%
10. they reproduce
11. upset
12. natural predators
13. 6, 10 days
14. lack of food
15. poison

Tribbles: Suggested discussion answers
1. When it endangers the lives or property of others.
2. They reproduce at a high rate consuming large amounts of food.
3. Answers will vary. (ex: armadillos, certain dogs, certain cats, kudzu, killer bees)
4. They can bring disease, and threaten native species and ecosystems.
5. Any living thing (plant or animal) that was not naturally found in an area.
6. No, the horse and the potato are exotics to North America.
7. They should be evaluated and harmful ones should be destroyed.
8. They should not have been allowed on the ship until the animal was fully understood.
9. Plants, bacteria, fungi.
10. Birds, cats, dogs, reptiles, and fish.

Qualitative Testing of Carbon Dioxide A Pollutant

1. Prepare Limewater: mix together about 3 cups of distilled or deionized water with 3 teaspoons of soda lime and let settle. Pour the cleared liquid into three glasses for testing. Avoid having any of the left over soda lime in the glasses.
2. Fill a small plastic garbage bag half way with plain air. Place a straw in the neck of the bag and use the straw to "blow" bubbles out of the bag into the limewater. Observe the cloudiness of the limewater solution.
3. Now fill the plastic garbage bag half way with your exhaled breath. Place a straw in the neck of the bag and use the straw to blow bubbles into the limewater. Observe the cloudiness.
4. Catch some car exaust into your plastic bag (1/2 full). Place a straw in the neck of the bag and use the straw to blow bubbles into your limewater. Observe the cloudiness.

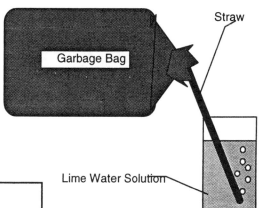

Limewater reacts with the carbon dioxide in the air and becomes cloudy. The more carbon dioxide present the more cloudy it will become.

Compare the relative concentrations of carbon dioxide in your three samples of gas.

Observations:

Carbon Dioxide levels in the Earth's Atmosphere
Approximate Levels
(in parts per million (ppm))

Year	PPM	Year	PPM
1870	291	1974	328
1900	287	1976	330
1920	303	1978	333
1930	310	1980	337
1960	315	1982	340
1965	320	1983	342
1970	325	1985	345
		1989	349

Graph the above data on the area to the right. Have the years axis go from 1850 to 2050. Draw the best fit line for the data and extrapolate to the year 2050. Overall, what has happened to the Carbon Dioxide levels (over the 200 year period)?

Graph of Carbon Dioxide levels over 200 year period

135

Geology

Jurassic Park
Monolith Monsters

Activities:
Crystal Systems,
Fossil Formation

JURASSIC PARK
Teacher Information

Content Areas:
Dinosaur: biology, habitats, extinction, genetics; geology: fossils, amber, paleontology; genetic engineering, cryonics, chaos mathematics.

Synopsis:
Scientists using DNA extracted from fossils recreate dinosaurs, which are raised on an island for a tourist attraction. Without full understanding of the problems of bringing extinct species to life people lose control of the dinosaurs and must try to escape from the park.

Good Science:
DNA can be extracted from fossils
It is possible to put the DNA of one animal into the embryo of another.
The sizes and characteristics of the dinosaurs are correct as far as science knows today.
Chaos is a recognized branch of mathematics, and the comments made about chaos in the film
        are factual
The fossil dig at the beginning of the film is realistic.

Bad Science:
The velociraptor in the film is a mix of two different kinds of dinosaurs known.
It is not currently possible to extract enough DNA from a fossil to recreate an animal.
Grabbing hold of something that was just in liquid nitrogen would probably freeze fingers.

Other:
Jurassic Park can be purchased as a videotape or a videodisc (in both CAV and CLV formats).
You may wish to omit the following questionable language:
Side 1 CAV frames 31480 to 31500 Time: approximately at 17 min.
Side 2 CAV frames 35700 to 35750 Time: approximately at 50 min.

JURASSIC PARK

Directed by Steven Spielberg   *First shown in 1993*
Color   *2 hours 7 mins.*   *PG-13*
Based on the book by Michael Crichton
Chaos with dinosaurs

Questions to be answered during the video:

1. The story takes place on an island which is off the coast of what country?

2. What kind of mine is being worked in the Dominican Republic?

3. What is encased in the yellow rock?

4. What tools are used to clear dirt from the buried bones?

5. The "radar" is shot into the ground to find what?

6. Dinosaurs have more in common with _____ than with reptiles.

7. The Cretaceous _____ was when Velociraptors lived.

8. Nedry promises to steal 15 viable _____, one of each species.

9. What branch of mathematics does the mathematician study?

10. Give an example of one of the security features on the island.

11. How long is the neck on the Brachyosaurus?

12. How fast can a Tyrannosaurus Rex run?

13. "They do move in _____."

14. What do the scientists extract from 100 million year old dinosaur blood?

15. DNA is the _____ of life.

16. What material is fossilized to form amber?

17. What is the robot arm doing to the eggs?

18. What prevents the dinosaurs from breeding in the park?

19. Velociraptors are (carnivores or herbivores).

20. What did the Velociraptors do that made people think they are intelligent?

21. "_____ is the most awesome force the world has ever seen."

22. How many years separated the existence of dinosaurs and man?

23. What specialized method does a Dilophosaurus use in hunting?

24. What is chaos?

25. What are the scientists using the Triceratops' droppings to find out?

26. What is the T-Rex vision based on?

27. What do the people see that let them know the dinosaur is coming?

28. Brachyosaurs are (carnivores or herbivores), because they only eat plants.

29. How do the people know the dinosaurs are breeding?

30. Lysine is an _____ acid, necessary for life, and it has been left out of the dinosaurs
    in the park.

31. The Gallimimus move in uniform motion, like a _____ evading a predator.

32. How can the people tell that the electric fence is off?

33. What happens when the Velociraptors exhale on the window?

Jurassic Park: Vocabulary
1. Amber	2. Amino acid	3. Carnivore
4. Chaos	5. Chromosome	6. Clone
7. Dinosaur	8. DNA	9. Embryo
10. Extinct	11. Fossil	12. Genetic
13. Herbivore	14. Predator	15. Raptor

Jurassic Park: Discussion questions

1. What are some possible reasons for choosing that island for the Jurassic Park?

2. What characteristics of the western United States contribute to the preservation of dinosaur remains?

3. In the film, a type of radar was used (actually it's sonar) to find a dinosaur fossil. How can sound be used to locate objects?

4. With today's technologies it is possible to freeze animal embryos. Describe some reasons or purposes why we would want to.

5. In the film not only were dinosaurs brought back into existence, the scientist also brought back extinct plants from the dinosaur period. Why might this become a problem?

6. Why would the name "Mesozoic Park" be a more accurate name for the movie than "Jurassic Park"?

7. What possible physical characteristics would people use to determine the intelligence of a fossilized animal?

8. Since the Velociraptor's breath condensed on the window, what can you conclude about its physiology?

Jurassic Park: *Answers to video questions*

1. Costa Rica
2. Amber
3. Mosquito
4. Paint brushes, small picks, hands
5. Location of fossils
6. Birds
7. Period
8. Embryos
9. Chaos
10. Electric fences, moat, motion sensors, the island itself
11. 25-27 feet
12. 32 MPH
13. Herds
14. DNA
15. Blueprint or building block
16. Tree sap
17. Turning
18. They are all engineered to be female
19. Carnivores
20. Tested the fences, learned
21. Genetics
22. 65 million
23. Poison venom, spitting.
24. Unpredictability
25. What it had eaten
26. Movement
27. Vibrations in the water
28. Herbivores
29. Hatched egg shells
30. Amino
31. Flock of birds
32. Lights were off, and the stick did not burn.
33. Condensation forms

Jurassic Park: *Suggested discussion answers*

1. Isolation of the newly created island species from mainland species
2. Dry climate, ground has not been disturbed, but has been geologically uplifted.
3. Echolocation: the sound reflects back from objects of certain density.
4. Preservation of species from extinction, assist in reproduction.
5. Plants could get off the island and compete with existing plant life, plants could also be toxic.
6. Mesozoic era encompasses all of the time that dinosaurs lived while Jurassic is only a period of that era.
7. Brain size to body size ratio, size and shape of brain area.
8. Warm blooded.

Jurassic Park Dinosaurs

Time: Cretaceous; 69 MYA
Length: 18-25 ft. Weight 3-6 tons
Speed 35 mph.
Habitat: Wet forests
Herbivore. Traveled in herds

For each of the dinosaurs shown from the film match the name to the dinosaur silhouette.
The movie tried to be very accurate with its portrayal of dinosaurs. The only real exceptions were that the dilophasaurus was larger than in the film, and many of the dinosaurs shown did not exist at the same time.

Time: Cretaceous; 74 MYA
Length: 30 ft. Weight: 2-4 tons
Speed: 35+ mph
Habitat: Forests & meadows
Herbivore. Traveled in herds

Time: Cretaceous; 75 MYA
Length 6-9 ft. Weight 60-140 lbs
Speed: 35 to 40 mph.
Habitat: Deserts to forests
Carnivore: Pack hunters

Triceratops

Tyrannosaurus Rex

Gallimimus

Velociraptor

Dilophosaurus

Mosquito

Brachiosaurus

Parasaurolophus
(Trombone Duckbill)

Time: Cretaceous; 66 MYA
Length: 40-50 ft. Weight 3-5 tons
Speed: 35-40 mph
Habitat: Forests, brush & swamp
Carnivore. Small groups/alone

Time: Jurassic; 145 MYA
Length: 100 ft. Weight: 40 tons
Speed: 20 mph tops
Habitat: Floodplains near rivers
Herbivore. Large herds

Time: Late Triassic, 212 MYA
Length: 2-3 ft.Weight 10-20 lbs.
Speed: 33 mph
Habitat: Conifer forests
Carnivore. Traveled in packs

Time: Cretaceous; 69 MYA
Length: 15-20 ft. Weight 300-600 lbs
Speed: 50 mph
Habitat: Dunes, swampy forests, meadows

Note: MYA means Million Years Ago

Dinosaur is actually a Latin word that means "Terrible Lizard" and were first discovered in Sussex, England in 1822 by Gideon Mantell

Not actually a dinosaur:
Time: Devonian to present
Oldest fossil: 390 MYA
2600 species   Carnivore
Habitat: Worldwide except extremes

MONOLITH MONSTERS
Teacher Information

Content Areas:
Meteors, geology, crystals, elements, chemical properties, medical technology.

Synopsis:
A meteorite containing crystals with strange properties crashes onto the Earth. The crystals are discovered to absorb all silicates in the presence of water. The crystals, when wet, grow to giant proportions, then fall and crush anything in their path. To stop the crystals from destroying the town, a geologist discovers that the crystal growth is halted by salt water.

Good Science:
The explanation about meteors at the beginning of the film is excellent.
Some minerals do have properties that change in the presence of water.
The use of the "iron lung" for patients of that time is correct.
The proper methods for determining the identification of a rock are presented correctly.
Great salt flats are the remnants of ancient oceans.

Bad Science:
There is no known crystal that absorbs and grows as the one shown.
If salt water stops the crystals from growing, then humans (filled with saline water) would not be
      affected.

Other:
A rock sold as the "popcorn rock" does grow crystals when placed in a shallow dish of water.

MONOLITH MONSTERS

Directed by John Sherwood   First shown in 1957
Black & White   1 hour 18 minutes
Killer rocks from space

Questions to be answered duringthe video:

1. Earth is bombarded by _____.

2. What happens to most meteors that come in contact with the Earth's atmosphere?

3. What is formed from the collision of a meteor and the Earth's crust?

4. In what type of climate did the driver find the rock?

5. "If you look closely you can see _____ in the rock."

6. What did the salt flats used to be?

7. Ben and Dave have what profession?

8. What happens when the rock encounters water?

9. What happened to Ben?

10. Why is the doctor sending Ben's body to the state medical examiner?

11. What happened to the Simpson's house?

12. Using a microscope Dave sees that the rock has a negative _____.

13. What common substance is the rock made of?

14. Why does Jenny need to go to the hospital?

15. What does Dr. Flanders say the rock is?

16. What does Dr. Flanders notice around the rocks on the ground?

17. What material is missing from the wreckage and the dirt sample?

18. Silicon in the body is a _____ element.

19. What does the theory say that silicon does in the body?

20. What is the shape of the growing rock?

21. What compound causes the rocks to react and grow?

22. What do Dave & Dr. Flanders want to do to the town?

23. Why does Dave want the formula that the doctor used on Jenny?

24. What has the governor declared around the town of San Angelo?

25. What is a saline solution?

26. How does Dave want to stop the monoliths?

27. "In _____ there are no guarantees."

28. How strong of a solution is needed to stop the monoliths?

Monolith Monsters: Vocabulary

1. Catalyst	2. Cleavage	3. Crystal
4. Dormant	5. Meteor	6. Mixture
7. Monolith	8. Petrified	9. Saline
10. Solution	11. Speed	12. Synthetic
13. Tektite	14. Trace	

Monolith Monsters: Discussion questions

1. What do you think is the purpose of an iron lung?

2. What would have happened if the meteor had fallen into the ocean?

3. Why wouldn't the monoliths in the back of the group keep growing?

4. If over 1,000,000 tons of meteor material fall to the Earth's surface each year, why don't you find meteors all the time?

5. Many materials that are sold are expressed in percent solution. Milk is often sold as 2% milk fat. This means that there are two grams of fat for every 100 grams of milk. What is the percent solution of salt water if you dissolve 50 grams of salt in 1 liter (1000 g) of water?

6. How long would it take the monoliths to get to the town if the town was one mile (5280 feet) from the approaching edge of the monoliths, keeping in mind that monoliths take about 10 min. to grow to their full height of 100 feet before they fall down?

Monolith Monsters: Answers to video questions

1. meteors
2. burn up to dust
3. craters
4. desert/dry
5. strata
6. an ocean
7. geologists
8. bubbles and foams
9. died, and became stiff
10. because he can't figure out what happened to Ben
11. demolished
12. cleavage
13. silica
14. she is turning to stone
15. a meteor
16. the ground is discolored, lifeless
17. silicates
18. trace
19. make it flexible
20. crystal
21. water
22. evacuate
23. to try it on the rocks and see if it stops them from growing
24. a state of emergency
25. a salt (sodium chloride) solution (dissolved in water)
26. blow up the dam and make a salt-water barrier
27. science
28. 3%

Monolith Monsters: Suggested discussion answers

1. An iron lung is a machine that makes it possible for a person to breathe, when they can no longer do it for themselves. By lowering the pressure inside the "lung" it causes the person's lungs to inflate, and by increasing the pressure inside the person's lungs deflate.
2. According to the film nothing. Since saltwater stopped the monoliths, falling into the ocean's saltwater would have neutralized their effect.
3. The monoliths in the back could not grow because they had already used up all of the available silicon.
4. Most meteors that meet the Earth's atmosphere are about the size of a grain of sand, they, in part, make up the dust that is found in the atmosphere.
5. Percent solution = (grams of solute/grams of solution) x 100
   50g salt/1050 g salt water = 0.047 (100) = 4.7%
6. Speed = distance/time therefor time = distance/speed
   If the monoliths grow to 100 feet and then fall down every 10 min. they are moving forward at a speed of [100 feet/10 min. =] 10 feet/min.
   So to get to town it will take [5280 feet/(10 feet/min.)] = 528 min. (8.8 hrs).

Crystal Systems

Most minerals form from liquids, a process which allows the atoms to arrange themselves geometrically, producing crystals. If a mineral is allowed to grow freely it will develop a crystal shape. The crystal shape is an important clue to identifying a mineral, and geologists recognize six different crystal systems, based on crystal structure (shape). The sides of a crystal are termed faces, and these meet one another in the interfacial angle. A crystal hardly ever is left alone enough to grow evenly. Sometimes one face grows faster than another and the end result crystal looks nothing like its theoretical type. But the *law of constancy of interfacial angles* states that angles between the faces are always the same no matter how distorted the crystal may be. The interfacial angles of a crystal can be measured with a device called a goniometer.

The Six Crystal Systems

Cubic

Tetragonal

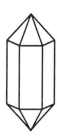
Hexagonal

Materials:
Alum (aluminum potassium sulfate)
Monofilament fishing line
Clear glasses (or paper or plastic cups)
Warm Distilled water
Silicon cement
Stirring rod or swizzle stick

In this activity you will grow alum crystals from a supersaturated alum solution. Alum can be purchased in almost any drug store.
1. Create a good seed crystal of alum by dissolving some alum in a small amount of water in a small glass or cup. Allow the water to evaporate (may take a few days). Small crystals will form on the sides and bottom of the glass.

2. Remove one of the crystals (this will be your seed crystal) of alum from the glass and attach it to a short length of monofilament fishing line with a small drop of silicon cement. Attach the other end of the fishing line to the middle of a pencil or small stick (long enough to cross the top of your glass).

3. Make your supersaturated crystal solution by dissolving the powdered alum in a glass of <u>warm</u> distilled water. How much alum you can dissolve depends on the temperature and amount of water. The best way to make the solution is to dissolve as much alum as you can and have just a small amount in the glass left undissolved. Then add some more warm water and dissolve what was left in the glass. It is important that there is no solid left in the glass.

4. Allow the crystal solution to cool, and then suspend your seed crystal in the crystal solution.

5. Allow the glass to sit somewhere where it will be undisturbed for several days. If your seed crystal disappears, dissolve more alum in the solution and suspend a new seed crystal. After a few days you should have a good sized crystal. Grow your crystal as large as you can, then measure the interfacial angles with your *goniometer.*

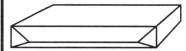
Orthorhombic

Monoclinic

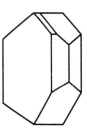
Triclinic

Build your own
Contact
Goniometer

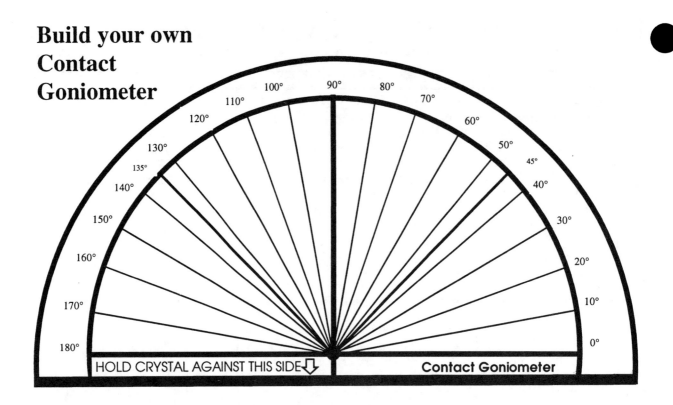

HOLD CRYSTAL AGAINST THIS SIDE ⬇   **Contact Goniometer**

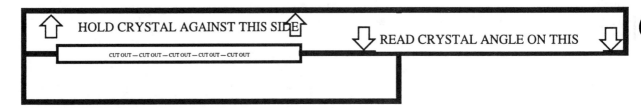

⬆ HOLD CRYSTAL AGAINST THIS SIDE ⬆   ⬇ READ CRYSTAL ANGLE ON THIS ⬇

CUT OUT — CUT OUT — CUT OUT — CUT OUT — CUT OUT

   A goniometer is a device that is used to measure the interfacial angles on a crystal. Simple goniometers like this contact goniometer measure the angles by touching. More sophisticated goniometers can mount the crystals on a rotating table, and reflect laser light off the faces, measuring the angle you have to turn the crystal to bring the next reflection into place.

   Make your Contact Goniometer by carefully cutting out the above diagrams and pasting them onto stiff cardboard. Cut out the middle section of the measuring arm, and poke a hole in the black circle of the graduated back. Use a paper fastener to hold the measuring arm onto the graduated back.

   Using any large crystal, measure the angle between the faces, by holding the crystal along the bottom of the graduated back, and rotating the measuring arm up to the crystal and then reading the angle.

Fossil Formation

Paleontologists study the life history of the Earth using fossils. **Fossils** are evidence (traces or remains) of previous living things. Fossils are useful in finding out about animals, plants, and the environment as they were in the past. Fossils can also be used to approximate the time when rocks were formed by using fossils of animals or plants that only existed for a certain period of time as index fossils. There are six main types of fossils, classified by how they are formed. **Whole Animal** (or Organism) is a fossil with an entire organism preserved within a material that has turned to rock (insect in amber). **Petrification** is where the original material has been replaced by mineral substances (petrified wood). **Molds** occur when a buried organism dissolves away leaving a cavity of its exact shape. **Casts** happen when mold cavities fill with new minerals. **Trace** fossils are formed when an organism leaves marks or other evidence of the organism, or its activities (foot prints). **Imprint** fossils are formed when a thin object (e.g. leaf, feather) becomes trapped in soft material which later becomes rock, leaving the object's impression even after the surrounding material has become stone.

Materials:
Plaster of Paris
Spray vegetable oil
Styrofoam or paper bowl
Branch from a fern or
    other small leafy
    branch

ImprintFossil

1. Mix a small bowl's worth of plaster of paris according to the directions on the package.
2. Coat the inside of the bowl with oil.
3. Pour a thin layer of plaster into the bowl (1-2 centimeters).
4. Allow the plaster some time to settle and begin to harden.
5. Lightly press your leafy stem into the plaster.
6. Allow the plaster to harden completely, and then remove your branch.
7. Spray oil over the top of your plaster.
8. Pour another thin layer of plaster on top of the oil on the first layer.
10. After the plaster has hardened, you can separate the two layers and see the imprint fossils you created.

Whole Animal Fossil

In this activity you will simulate an insect in amber.

Materials:
Hobby polyester
    resin kit
Small paper cups
Dead insect
Stirring stick

1. Mix a small amout of liquid resin and its hardener, according to the directions on the package. **Be extra careful using the resin kit and follow all precautions.**
2. Pour a small amout of the resin into the bottom of a small paper cup.
3. Gently place a dead insect (or small leaf or other object) onto the resin in the paper cup.
4. Add more resin to the cup until the resin completely covers your insect.
5. Once the resin has completely hardened, peel off the paper cup.
6. You now have your fossil.

Marine Science:

It Came from Beneath the Sea
Jaws

Activity:
Using Fish Anatomy to Determine
Habitat,
Shark Key,
Squid Dissection

IT CAME FROM BENEATH THE SEA
Teacher Information

Content Areas:
Squid biology, octopus behavior and intelligence, atomic testing, radiation, loss of habitat.

Synopsis:
Due to atomic testing a giant mollusk must search for new food sources (people). The navy responding to this threat attempts to kill the giant creature with high voltage and explosive harpoons.

Good Science:
There are giant squid. (debate still continues on size)
The octopus is indeed one of the most intelligent invertebrates, and can solve puzzles by itself.
Through exploration and testing man has caused many plants and animals to lose or be unable to
       adapt to their habitat.

Bad Science:
Giant squid and giant octopus do not attack people.
An animal that highly radioactive would have a hard time surviving (death due to radiation
       poisoning)
If you look very carefully you should note that the octoput has only six arms.

Follow Up
Have the students watch the documentary:
       National Geographic's "Cousteau's the Octopus"

IT CAME FROM BENEATH THE SEA

Directed by Robert Gordon   *First shown in 1955*
Black & White   80 min.
Giant Octopus Attacks San Francisco

Questions to be answered during the video:

1. How is the submarine powered?

2. What instrument/equipment was used to find the target following the submarine?

3. What object was stuck in the submarine's bow plane?

4. In what field is Professor Joyce an expert?

5. What is not allowed on submarines?

6. What is the monster?

7. Some Giant Squids have been found over _____ feet long.

8. Why do the scientists think that the monster came up from the depths of the ocean?

9. What do the scientists think happened to the octopus that scared away his food source? He

   became _____

10. How does the Polar Empress survivor describe what happened?

11. What is the body of an octopus like?

12. Describe the marks found in the sand:

13. What happens to the sheriff?

14. What is Dr. Joyce's reaction to a crisis?

15. In what city are the operational headquarters located?

16. How is the submarine net supposed to repel or kill the "monster"?

17. What is the octopus's only vital spot?

18. In what century do records show that a similar monster attacked towns?

19. Where is the monster from in the Pacific?

20. What does the high voltage do to the octopus?

21. What does the Navy want done around the ferry area?

22. What do they use to drive the octopus back into the water?

23. What does the octopus after being hit with the torpedo?

24. What does the Captain use to shoot the octopus?

25. Where does the scientist shoot the octopus?

It Came From Beneath the Sea: Vocabulary

1. Atomic
2. Biologist
3. Cephalopod
4. Harpoon
5. Octopus
6. Radiation
7. Reactor
8. SONAR
9. Squid
10. Trench (oceanic)

It Came from Beneath the Sea: Discussion questions

1. Look up in an encyclopedia and get information on the
     a: Giant Squid
     b: Pacific Giant Octopus

2. In the video the scientist talked about the octopus learning. How smart do you think an octopus is? (look it up)

3. The reason given for why the monster octopus moved was man's encroachment on its living area. This is called "loss of habitat." Describe a local example of an animal moving because of loss of habitat.

4. Can you think of any land animal that can lift part of its body without a rigid bony structure?

5. If the monster octopus was radioactive is it reasonable to think it could have survived as long as it did?

6. The film said that some animals can sense radiation, a sense we don't have. Find an animal that can sense these things that people can't:
     a. ultrasonics
     b. subsonics
     c. electric fields
     d. magnetic fields
     e. movement pressure in the water

     v. dog
     w. elephant
     x. shark
     y. whales
     z. fish

It Came From Beneath the Sea: Answers to video questions
1. atomic/nuclear
2. sonar
3. living tissue
4. marine biology
5. women
6. an octopus
7. 100
8. atomic bomb testing
9. radioactive
10. something came up and grabbed the ship
11. water filled sack
12. round shallow depressions
13. he gets eaten
14. she screams (not very cool in a crisis is she?)
15. San Fransisco
16. high voltage electricity
17. its brain
18. 13th
19. Mickanile Deep
20. make it come out of the water/ attack the bridge
21. evacuate
22. heat/fire
23. attacks the submarine
24. explosive harpoon
25. the eye

It Came from Beneath the Sea: Suggested discussion answers
1. Answers will vary.
2 Answers will vary. But the octopus is a very smart animal, and is the most intelligent of the invertebrates.
3. Answers will vary. Example: Snakes, turtles, and nesting birds moving out of an area as it is developed.
4. An elephant's trunk and a person's tongue both lack bone structure.
5. No, constant exposure to large amounts of radiation would form mutations such as cancers.
6. a-v, b-w, c-x, d-y, e-z

JAWS
Teacher Information

Content Areas:
Shark biology, shark behavior, oceanography.

Synopsis:
A great white shark starts attacking people in a resort community during a holiday season. The chief of police with an oceanographer and a local fisherman go out to hunt and kill the shark.

Good Science:
Great white sharks actually grow to the size shown.
Great whites have attacked people and do inhabit all oceans.
People do study sharks using shark cages.
Many sharks can drown if they can't swim (to keep water flowing over their gills).

Bad Science:
The behavior of the shark during an attack. During most shark attacks the shark bites and then lets go of the person, it does not hold on and play with its food.

Other:
There are many shark documentaries available to use for comparison and information.
Sharks known as "dogfish" are available from science suppliers.

JAWS

Directed by Steven Spielberg   *First shown in 1975*
Color   2hrs 4min
Based on the novel by Peter Benchley

Questions to be answered during the video:

1. How does the shark attack the first victim?

2. What is the reason for the sun coming in the window now?

3. Why does the man's wife call him "Chief"?

4. Where does the story take place?

5. What washed up on the beach after the shark attack?

6. Why does the Chief want "Beach Closed" signs?

7. What does the town's medical examiner want to change the girl's reported cause of death to

    be?

8. How does Harry describe the water?

9. What were the next two shark attack victims?

10. Why don't the people want the beach closed?

11. What were the two men at the pier trying to do?

12. When Hooper from the Oceanographic Institute inspects the remains of the first victim, what

    does he think is the cause of death?

13. What kind of shark was caught?

14. Why does Hooper think that the caught shark is not the killer?

15. Is the caught shark a man eating shark?

16. What is the water depth in which most shark attacks occur?

17. When the shark is cut open, is it the one who killed the people?

18. What happened to Ben Gardner's boat?

19. What did Hooper find in Ben Gardner's boat other than Ben?

20. What are sharks attracted to at the beach?

21. Hooper says all that sharks do is _____ and have _____.

22. What is wrong with the Chief's son after the shark attack in the pond?

23. What is the purpose of the shark cage?

24. What is in Hooper's tanks?

25. What are the estimates of the shark's size?

26. What it the purpose of the yellow barrels?

27. What kind of shark attacked the crew of the Indianapolis?

28. What is the wailing sound heard?

29. Why does the boat try to lead the shark into shallow water?

30. When Hooper is in the shark cage, what is he trying to do to the shark?

31. How does the shark catch Capt. Quint?

32. How does Chief Brody kill the shark?

JAWS: Vocabulary
1. Laceration	2. Predator	3. Prey
4. Silhouette	5. Velocity	6. Symmetrical
7. Accelerate	8. Serrate	9. Thorax
10. Alimentary canal	11. Rogue	12. Territoriality
13. Cartilage		

JAWS: Discussion questions
1. Label the following shark parts:

a. dorsal fin	b. pectoral fin	c. anal fin	d. second dorsal fin
e. caudal fin	f. gills	h. lateral line	i. eye
j. nostril	k. ampullae of lorenzini		

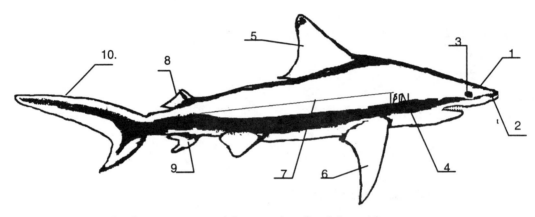

2. Which of the above shark parts are used for sensing food (prey)?

3. What would be the normal food sources for a Great White Shark?

4. From the movie what are the steps or procedures that a shark goes through in deciding if something is food? (is this realistic?)

5. The hand washed up on the beach is higher than the intertidal zone. Why is this impossible?

6. Since sharks are cartilaginous fish, what damage would have occurred to the shark as it jumped onto the boat?

7. Do you feel that beaches should be closed, as Chief Brody did, after a single shark attack? Why?

8. Since most shark attacks occur at the surface, in shallow water (3 feet) or near shore (within 10 feet), what are the conditions that the shark is experiencing while sensing its food?

9. Would the loss of a tooth interfere with a shark's ability to feed? (Why or why not?)

10. How is it possible to drown a shark?

JAWS: Answers to video questions

1. attacks from below, bites her legs
    and pulls her under
2. change of season to summer
3. he is Chief of Police
4. Amity Island
5. a hand
6. to protect the people from shark attacks
7. a boating accident
8. cold
9. the dog (Pippet) and the boy (Alex)
10. they don't want to lose tourist and money
11. catch the shark
12. shark attack
13. tiger shark
14. wrong bite radius
15. yes
16. 3 feet deep, 10 feet from shore
17. no
18. sunk
19. a shark tooth
20. splashing
21. eat and make baby sharks
22. shock
23. to protect a diver from sharks
24. compressed air
25. 20 to 25 feet long
26. locate the shark and keep it from diving
27. tiger shark
28. whale song
29. to drown the shark
30. poison the shark
31. jumps onto the back of the boat and
    Quint slides into the shark mouth.
32. puts a compressed air tank into the
    sharks mouth and shoots the tank,
    blowing up the shark.

Jaws: Suggested discussion answers

1. 1:k, 2:j, 3:i, 4:f, 5:a, 6:b, 7:h, 8:d, 9:c, 10:e
2. h, i, j, k
3. Great white sharks usually eat fish and marine mammals.
4. The steps are: a. sensing nearness of prey; b. bump, touching of prey; c. bite, taste of prey; d. eat. The behavior of this shark seems very unrealistic: it seems to "play" with its food; it seems to hold its prey up for observation; it jumps onto a boat (an act which would kill a shark); overall while the shark has a very real "appearance" it has very poor "behavior."
5. Since the tide does not go above the intertidal zone there is no way for the body parts to be carried to that point.
6. It would have damaged (ruptured) its interior organs thereby killing itself.
7. Answers will vary.
8. These conditions would cause objects to be seen in silhouette, water is cloudy, and hearing is difficult because of surf noise.
9. No. Sharks have multiple rows of teeth to replace those lost.
10. Sharks must move to breathe, most lack the ability to pull water over their gills, so if they get stuck they can't breathe (drown).

Using Fish Anatomy to Determine Habitat

Find a marine fish in a grocery store, a caught ocean fish, or even a picture of an ocean fish. Draw a rough diagram of the fish on the back of this paper. Analyze the marine fish's anatomy to determine its habitat. Carefully examine the different parts of the fish's anatomy taking one characteristic at a time. Choose from the anatomical choices which correspond to your fish, and label the choice on your fish diagram. When you have finished, write a short summary paragraph describing the habitat of your fish. Look up in a reference book about your fish's habitat and compare it to your summary.

1. Color: the color of a fish can determine whether the fish lives near the top or bottom or if it is a reef fish.
   - **Silver colored:** a swimming fish that is camouflaged from animals below.
   - **Blue green or dark tops:** camouflaged from above, fish lives near bottom.
   - **Sandy colored:** bottom dweller.
   - **Colorful:** reef dweller or poisonous.

2. Body Shape: the shape of the fish's body can indicate its environment.
   - **Very Thin:** live near a reef where they can escape.
   - **Long and Slender**: fast swimmers, open ocean dwellers.
   - **Large Heads and Tapered Bodies:** slow swimmers and bottom dwellers.

3. Tail or Caudal Fin: an indication of swimming behavior and capability.
   - **Forked Shaped:** fastest swimmers.
   - **Rounded Tail:** slow swimmers.

4. Mouth: the size and location of the fish's mouth can indicate behavior.
Size:
   - **Large mouth**: fish can eat large prey and gulp large amounts of water, increasing oxygen intake.
   - **Small mouth:** fish can eat small prey or are herbivores.

Location:
   - **Upturned Mouth:** lives near the surface.
   - **Mouth Near Middle:** lives in mid-level of water.
   - **Mouth Near Bottom:** bottom dweller.

5. Eyes: location of the eyes can indicate the fish's behavior.
   - **Both Eyes on One Side:** bottom dweller.

Shark Key

Sharks come in a variety of shapes and sizes. There are currently over 296 different types of sharks known. Some sharks are very big (over 25 feet long), but most sharks are under three feet in length.

Use the following questions to identify the sharks pictured. Answer each question with a yes or no response, then follow the directions or identifications that follow your answer. This format is called a dichotomous key, meaning that there are only two possible choices for an answer.

1. Does the shark have an unusual shaped head?
   YES: go to question 2   *NO*: go to question 4

2. Does the shark have a diamond shaped body?
   YES: its an **Angel Shark**   *NO*: go to 3

3. Does the shark have a wide flattened head, with a regular shaped body?
   YES: **Hammerhead Shark**   *NO*: go back to 1: you made a mistake

4. Does the shark's caudal fin have a lower lobe?
   YES go to 5   *NO*: **Nurse Shark**

5. Is the upper lobe of the caudal fin at least twice as big as the lower lobe?
   YES: go to 6   *NO*: go to 9

6. Is the upper lobe of the caudal fin as long as the shark's body?
   YES: **Thresher Shark**   *NO*: go to 7

7. Does the shark appear to have stripes on its upper body?
   YES: **Tiger Shark**   *NO*: go to 8

8. Does the shark have a long thin cigar shaped body?
   YES: **Blue Shark**   *NO*: go back to 1: you made a mistake

9. Does the shark have a thick body with an upturned snout?
   YES: **Great White Shark**   *NO*: go to 10

10. Does the shark's dorsal fin start above the pectoral fins, and does it have a   normal shaped body?
   YES: **Mackerel Shark**   *NO*: go back to 1: you made a mistake

Use the key to identify these sharks

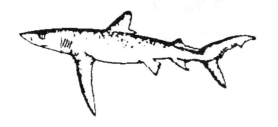

A.

B.

C.

D.

E.

F. top view

G.

H.

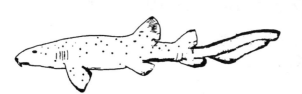

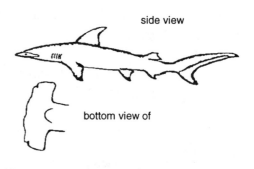

side view

bottom view of

Squid Dissection

Materials:
Squid
Small sharp
  scissors
Paper plate
Paper towels
Hand lens or
Magnifying glass

Squid are invertebrate marine animals from the class *Cephalopoda* (head footed), which is in the phylum *Mollusca*. Some of its closest relatives are the octopus, the cuttlefish, and the nautilus. The squid has an internal shell known as the pen, and moves through the water by means of jet propulsion using its siphon. Squid are often available from seafood markets and bait stores and are served in restaurants as *calimari*.

External Anatomy:
1. Lay your squid flat on a paper towel on a paper plate.
2. Draw in the space provided the squid's external structure and features, and indicate the length of your squid. Examine your squid carefully. Check off each of the items described below as you find them and label them on your drawing.

___ **Mantle** - the thick muscular layer that covers most of the body.

___ **Eyes**

___ **Siphon** - tube-like structure protruding out from under the mantle.

___ **Chromatophores** - freckles on the mantle (These are pigment cells that allow the squid to change color from white to purple to almost black, and may for communication and camouflage)

___ **Dorsal** (back) side - has two fins that help stabilize the squid when swimming and act as rudders for sudden turns.

___ **Fins**

___ **Ventral** (front) **side** - side with the siphon.

___ **Arms** - there are eight arms

___ **Tentacles** or grasping arms- there are two grasping arms.

___ **Suckers** _ located on the tentacles.

___ **Beak** (mouth) - separate the arms and find the mouth in the center.

Squid: External Anatomy Diagram

Internal Anatomy:

1. Lay your squid flat on a paper towel on the paper plate with the siphon up.
2. Carefully cut the mantle starting next to the siphon and going all the way to the posterior (back) tip. <u>Do not</u> cut the organs inside the squid.
3. Using the provided diagrams locate and check of the following features.

   ___ **Gills**. They are two feathery looking organs on either side of the body cavity.

   ___ **Branchial heart** - at the base of each gill, a small whitish bulblike structure (may be difficult to see)

   ___ **Liver** - large organ in the center of the squid's body.

   ___ **Ink sac** - black in color and has a tube leading toward the siphon.

   ___**Rectum** - right next to the ink sac, a very thin tube with an opening near the siphon.

   ___ **Gonads** - sex organs located at the posterior end of the body cavity. *(when sex of an animal is unknown the sex organs are called gonads).* The gonads will either be **ovaries** in females or **testis** in males. Determine whether your squid is male or female and put a check mark on the appropriate structure diagram.

   ___ **Pen** - stiff and plastic-like structure located toward the dorsal (back) side of the squid.

4. Using a hand lens or magnifying glass draw a picture of the gill's structure.
5. Carefully clip open the ink sac. Using the squid's ink, make a finger print or try to write your name in the space below.

Ink Sample

Male Squid Internal Anatomy

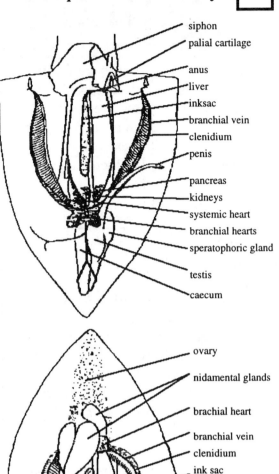

siphon
palial cartilage
anus
liver
inksac
branchial vein
clenidium
penis
pancreas
kidneys
systemic heart
branchial hearts
speratophoric gland
testis
caecum

ovary
nidamental glands
brachial heart
branchial vein
clenidium
ink sac
anus
pallial cartilage
siphon

Female Squid Internal Anatomy

Gill Diagram

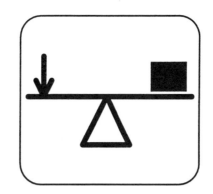

Physics:

Booby Trap
Destination Moon
Forbidden Planet

Activities:
Personal Radiation Dose,
Size of the Sun & Moon,
Free Fall and Forces,
Parallax Viewing

StarTrek®: The Next Generation: BOOBY TRAP
Teacher Information

Content Areas:

Radiation, inertia, impulse, gravity, modeling, energy, forces, physics.

Synopsis:

While answering a distress signal, the Enterprise becomes bombarded by radiation. As more energy is put out to escape the trap, more radiation put out to kill them. The crew discovers generators that convert their output energy into lethal radiation. Using modeling systems a method is discovered to escape, by using less energy.

Good Science:

Lethal dose limits of radiation, are determined by time, distance, and strength.
The more massive an object the greater its gravitational field and the more force it will
　　　exert on surrounding objects. Spacecraft do use the gravitational force of other
　　　planetary bodies to slingshot themselves into a new trajectory.
Modeling is a widely used method in science.

Bad Science:

There is no known way for a matter transporter system to work.
There is no known way to travel or communicate faster than light.
You can't blow up (input energy) generators that convert all forms of energy into radiation.

Other:

A solar panel would be a good example of an object that converts one form of energy into
　　　another form

StarTrek®: The Next Generation
BOOBY TRAP

Episode 53   Air Date 10/28/89
Color   46 Minutes
"Modeling as a method of experimentation"

Questions to be answered during the video:

1. What is the Enterprise receiving from the debris field?

2. What is the source of the signal?

3. What happens immediately after O'Brien transports the Captain?

4. After the Captain has returned to the Enterprise, what happened when the ship starts to leave?

5. What is the radiation field interfering with?

6. What was the reaction that occurred as the Enterprise changed its power output?

7. After shields fail how long until fatal exposure?

8. The magnetic coils are the alien Captain's _____.

9. How does the trap work?

10. Geordi wants to find a way to supplement the _____ supply to the ship and the engines.

11. The computer states that there would be a 9.73% margin of _____ for the interactions of the facsimile.

12. Aciton assimilators are _____ that convert energy into radiation.

13. Approximately how many assimilators are in the area?

14. How much of a weakness is present in one directional area?

15. What is the effect of the phasors on the assimilators?

16. There is a time _____ between force and counter force.

17. What could be fast enough to make the constant adjustments to overcome the outside generators?

18. Riker feels that "computers are good at taking orders, but not

_____."

19. What is Geordi's other way?

20. Name a factor that the computer can not take into account:

21. What are the units the velocity is expressed in after firing the thrusters?

22. What has reduced the ships velocity by 8%?

23. Ahead of the ship, what is the asteroid's gravitational field causing?

24. The captain used the asteroid's gravitational pull as a _____.

25. What does the crew of the Enterprise do to the booby trap?

Booby Trap: Vocabulary
1. Conservation
2. Force
3. Generator
4. Impulse (physics)
5. Inertia
6. Lethal
7. Model
8. Prototype
9. Simulation
10. Thrust
11. Vector
12. Velocity

Booby Trap: Discussion questions

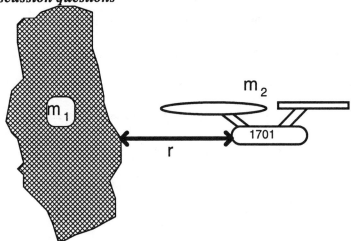

1. Newton's law of Universal Gravitation allows you to calculate the force between any two masses. The formula for calculating this force is $F = G (m_1 m_2)/r^2$; where G is the universal gravitational constant (6.67×10^{-11} N·m^2/kg^2), m_1 and m_2 are the masses in kilograms, and r is the distance between the masses in meters: using this formula will give you the force in Newtons (N). Estimating that the mass of the asteroid was 2.48×10^{16} kilograms and that the Enterprise has a mass of 4.96×10^9 kilograms, what was the force of attraction between them when the ship and asteroid were:

     a. 10 km (10,000 m) apart?

     b. 1 km (1,000 m) apart?

     c. 100 m apart?

2. What is the relationship between force due to gravity and distance?

3. Another of Newton's Laws is the 2nd Law of Motion, which states that force is equal to mass times acceleration (F=ma). By algebraically adjusting the formula this can also be stated as **a = F/m**. Using the information from question #1 what was the acceleration the Enterprise was experiencing when it was 1 kilometers from the asteroid? (pretend that the asteroid will not move)

4. List at least 3 advantages and 3 disadvantages of using a model to run an experiment instead of using the real thing.

5. Would blowing up the alien ship actually destroy the trap? (why or why not?)

Booby Trap: Answers to video questions
1. signal
2. battle cruiser
3. power drop
4. becomes bombarded by high radiation
5. scanners
6. opposing force increased
7. 30 minutes
8. log
9. the more energy they put out to escape the more force there is to kill them
10. energy (power)
11. error
12. generators
13. several hundred thousand
14. 0.1%
15. increasing radiation levels
16. delay
17. the ship's computer
18. creatively giving them
19. use less power to escape
20. intuition, experience, wish to stay alive
21. meters per second
22. gravitational attraction of the surrounding masses
23. increase velocity
24. slingshot
25. destroy it (blow it up)

Booby Trap: Suggested discussion answers
1.   a. 8.2×10^7 N

       b. 8.2×10^9 N

       c. 8.2×10^{11} N

2. There is an inverse square relationship. As the distance is doubled the force becomes 1/4 and as the distance is halved the force becomes four times as much.

3. At one kilometer from the asteroid the force would be 8.2×10^9 N, the mass of the Enterprise is 4.96×10^9 kilograms giving an acceleration of 1.65 m/s^2.

4. Answers will vary. Possible answers include: Advantages; easier to work will, save space and money, will not effect the real system: Disadvantages; not entirely accurate, may be missing variables, cost.

5. No, it would only destroy the bait, the generators would still be there.

DESTINATION MOON
Teacher Information
NSTA award winning lesson

Content Areas:
Gravitational forces, rocketry, magnetism, nuclear rockets, lunar conditions, freefall/weightlessness/microgravity.

Synopsis:
Private industry takes up the challenge to make the United States the first people to set foot on the moon. After constructing and traveling in a nuclear powered rocket to the moon, the crew find that they have used too much of their fuel. The crew strips the ship in order to lessen the ship's mass and increase their fuel efficiency and go home.

Good Science:
The depiction of conditions in space and on the moon are accurate.
The depiction of the behavior of objects in freefall orbit are accurate.
The processes about how nuclear rockets work shown are accurate.
The relationship between mass and fuel needed would be correct, and lightening the ship
     would allow the trip to be made with less fuel.

Bad Science:
The moon has dust over most of its surface, this is not shown in the film.

Other:
The Woody Woodpecker cartoon shown in the film, is an excellent film on its own about
     how rockets work, and conditions in space and on the moon.

DESTINATION MOON

Directed by Irving Pinchel   *First shown 1950*
Color   *91 min*   *Academy Award Winner: Special Effects*
Adapted from the novel "Rocketship Galileo" by Robert A. Heinlein

Questions to be answered during the video:

1. What happened to the first rocket shown?

2. How long have the people been working on the rocket?

3. How high did the scientist want to put a satellite?

4. Where is the next rocket going?

5. What kind of rocket engine will be used?

6. The shielding protects the crew from _____.

7. Who stars in the cartoon?

8. What do rockets use to fly?

9. How far is the Moon from Earth?

10. What is the escape velocity of the Earth?

11. The Moon has no _____.

12. What is the most important military fact of the century?

13. Why make the space suits bright colors?

14. What does the commission do to try and stop the rocket?

15. There is no law against doing _____.

16. Why can't Brown go on the trip?

17. Joe saw workers filling the rocket's fuel tanks with _____.

18. What happens to the men during take-off?

19. When are the people weightless?

20. What is special about the boots?

21. How do you think the people on the spaceship can tell where the cities are?

22. Why is the radar stuck?

23. Why can't you fall off a space ship?

24. How fast does the spaceship appear to be traveling?

25. How fast does the ship travel?

26. How did the man become "adrift"?

27. What do they use to save the man who "fell" off the ship?

28. How do they land the ship on the Moon?

29. For whom do the astronauts claim the Moon?

30. How much of a time lag is there between the Earth and Moon by radio?

31. What is the Moon's surface like?

32. How big does the Earth appear to be from the Moon?

33. What is the gravity on the Moon compared to that of the Earth?

34. What tool does the General use to investigate the rocks?

35. Why don't Joe and Cargraves know which way to look when the General calls?

36. How much does the telescope-camera weigh on Earth?

37. What does the crew do when they find out they don't have enough fuel to return?

38. Why would this help (see above question)?

39. What season is it in the United States on their return?

40. How can you tell what season it is?

Extra Credit: read the book that the movie was based on and write a one page report

outlining the difference between the book and the movie.

Destination Moon: Vocabulary

1. Aft
2. Accuracy
3. Accelerate
4. Appendicitis
5. Appropriation
6. Atomic
7. Escape velocity
8. Geiger counter
9. Gravity
10. Lateral
11. Orbit
12. Plane (surface)
13. Production
14. Propaganda
15. Radar
16. Radiation
17. Reaction mass
18. Research
19. Rocket
20. Thrust
21. Vacuum
22. Velocity

Destination Moon: Discussion questions

1. Why do people explore space?

2. How accurate do you think the movie is?

3. Is there a prejudiced or propagandistic view to the movie? If so what?

4. Why does the ship not appear to be moving while in space? Can you think of another

   example of this behavior?

5. What are the risks and benefits of space exploration?
6. How do you think that you have benefited from space exploration?

Destination Moon: Math questions

1) Convert 7 miles/second into miles/hour.

2.1) Why is there a three second time lag with a lunar discussion?

2.2) How long will it take light at a speed of 186,000 miles/sec to travel 240,000 miles?

3.1) What would a 200 pound person weigh on the moon?

3.2) What would be the weight of the telescope camera on the moon?

4.1) Convert the escape velocity of the Earth into feet/sec.?

4.2) What is the acceleration in feet/sec/sec, if it takes 2.5 min to achieve escape velocity?

4.3) What was the G-force then during take off?(1 G = 32 ft/s/s)

5.1) If the moon is 240,000 miles away and it takes 2 days to get there what is the average

   speed of the trip in miles/day?

5.2) What is the average speed in miles/hour?

Destination Moon: Answers to video questions

1. went off course and crashed, motor error, sabotage
2. 4 years
3. 12,000 miles
4. moon
5. atomic
6. radioactivity
7. Woody Woodpecker
8. jets, shotgun kick, action reaction
9. 240,000 miles
10. 7 miles/second
11. air, atmosphere
12. who controls the moon can control the Earth
13. for easy visibility and contrast
14. says they can't test the engine
15. launching a spaceship
16. appendicitis operation
17. water
18. sink into seats, yelling, face pulls back
19. free orbit, open space
20. magnets on bottoms
21. city lights
22. frozen grease
23. you are in the same orbit
24. it doesn't appear to be moving
25. thousands of miles per hour
26. he let his boot magnets lose contact with the ship
27. rope and an oxygen bottle
28. backwards, tail first, on automatic
29. all people of the Earth
30. rocky, barren, rough
31. 3 seconds
32. larger than the moon in our sky (actually 4 times larger)
33. 1/6
34. a Geiger counter
35. you can't tell direction from a radio signal
36. 500-600 pounds
37. strip the ship of as much mass as possible
38. a ship of less mass needs less total thrust to be moved
39. summer
40. tilt of the Earth causes the north pole to be completely illuminated.

Destination Moon: Suggested answers to discussion questions
1. Answers will vary.
2. Answers will vary (but the movie is very accurate, only mistake is lack of dust on moon's surface.
3. Yes. The movie put a vary positive outlook toward American Industry
4. There are no nearby objects to compare its motion to. If you are flying in a jet plane it is difficult to tell your speed.
5. Answers will vary.
6. Answers will vary. (cable TV, fire-resistant cloth, satellite communications, personal computer....)

Destination Moon: Answers to the math questions
1: 25,200 miles/hour
2.1: the speed of light and radio is a form of light
2.2: 1.29 seconds
3.1: 33 1/3 pounds
3.2: 83 - 100 pounds
4.1: 36960 feet/second
4.2: 246.4 feet/sec/sec
4.3: 7.7 g's
5.1: 120,000 miles/day
5.2: 5000 miles/hour average

FORBIDDEN PLANET
Teacher Information

Content Areas:
Nuclear energy, electrical energy, components of personality, robotics, intelligence.

Synopsis:
A rescue ship, sent to find survivors on a distant planet, finds only two survivors. The survivors have been using the nuclear technology of a now extinct race to enhance themselves and their conditions. As a side effect of using the alien technology to boost intelligence, a man's unconscious self takes form and attacks others.

Good Science:
Energy can take several forms.

Bad Science:
There is no known way to travel faster than light.

Other:
This film is based on Shakespeare's play "The Tempest".

FORBIDDEN PLANET

Directed by Fred McLeod Wilcox   *First shown in 1956*
Color   *Running Time 1:39*
This film is based on Shakespeare's play "The Tempest".
The Id, the Ego, and the other thing

Questions to be answered during the video:

1. The ship has a Hyperdrive engine which makes it able to go faster than the speed of

_____

2. What kind of a star is Altair?

3. Which of Altair's planets does the ship orbit?

4. How does the planet's gravity compare to Earth's?

5. Name a sign of civilization that may be seen from space:

6. Robby says, "Oxygen promotes _____"

7. How does Robby respond when he is told to do something that may hurt someone?

8. Dr. Morbius is a Philologist, which is an expert in

_____

9. What does Dr. Morbius say killed the rest of the people on the planet?

10. Why can't the people hear Alta's whistle?

11. What part of the ship was removed to allow the crew to communicate with the home base?

12. What force or energy was used to move the cook?

13. What takes Robby a week when making star sapphires?

14. The planet used to be the home of the _____.

15. What is special about the molecules of the Krell door?

16. What did the shock of the Krell machine apparently increase in Dr. Morbius?

17. Each meter on the wall measures _____ times more than the meter before it.

18. What kind of power source supplies energy for the Krell machine?

19. How does the crew try to protect the ship?

20. The plaster model shows that the creature appears to be counter to every law of adaptive _____.

21. How do the gunners know where the "thing" is?

22. When did the creature disappear?

23. The creature attacking the ship is an invisible being that can't be disintegrated by _____

24. What is the Id?

25. Who made the monster?

26. As the creature heats up the metal door, what color change occurs with the metal?

27. When Commander Adams throws the switch, what kind of reaction does he start in the Krell furnace which cannot be reversed?

28. What happened to the planet?

Forbidden Planet Vocabulary

1. Atomic	2. Biped	3. Chain reaction
4. Density	5. Ego	6. Evolution
7. Force	8. Fusion	9. Id
10. Isotope	11. Pitch	12. Radar
13. Reactor	14. Ultrasonic	

Forbidden Planet: Discussion questions

1. What would be needed to make a body decompose on another planet?

2. If a planet blew up in exactly twenty four hours and you went 100 million miles away, why wouldn't you see it at the end of those 24 hours? (clue: light travels at 186,000 miles/second)

3. Name an energy conversion that occurs during the film: (example sunlight into chemical in plants)

4. If the robot is programmed not to hurt humans, what would be another good rule for robots?

5. What do you think are problems that need to be solved to travel at the speed of light (according to Einstein's theories an object cannot go the speed of light because it would take an infinite force)

6. Why is the planet called Altair 4?

7. Since our sun's name is Sol, what could be another name for our planet?

8. Since the gravity on Altair 4 was .897g's, what would be the weight of a person who weighed 100 pounds on Earth?

9. What was wrong with the animals shown, if they were taken from the earth 200,000 years ago?

10. The weapons were shooting neutron beams. What would neutron beams be? Could they be dangerous?

11. If a nuclear furnace is like a nuclear reactor, would looking into it with a mirror be safe? (why or why not?)

Label the parts of a nuclear power plant
1. control rods
2. nuclear fuel
3. outer containment shell
4. steel liner
5. core
6. steam generator
7. water pump

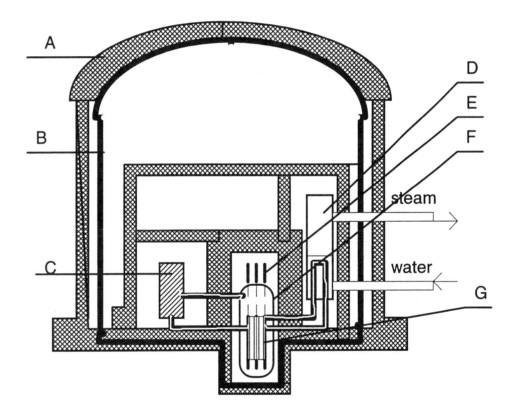

Forbidden Planet: Answers to video questions

1. light
2. main sequence star Altair
3. 4th planet
4. gravity .897
5. roads, city, dams
6. rust
7. Robby breaks down
8. expert in words and languages
9. a planetary force
10. it's above the pitch of human hearing
11. removed the ship's power core
12. electromagnetic
13. crystallizing
14. Krell
15. are densely locked and drink up energy
16. intelligence
17. 10 times
18. 9200 thermonuclear reactors
19. energy fence
20. evolution
21. radar
22. when Dr. Morbius woke up
23. nuclear fusion
24. subconscious mind
25. Dr. Morbius
26. red hot then white hot
27. chain reaction
28. blew up

Forbidden Planet: Suggested discussion answers

1. Bacteria, fungus, or some form of chemical decomposition.
2. Light would take some amount of extra time to travel that 100 million miles, so you wouldn't see it until 537.6 seconds after the 24 hours
3. Nuclear into mechanical, electrical into light, nuclear into electric, chemical into mechanical....
4. Answers will vary.
5. Answers will vary.
6. It is the fourth planet from the star Altair.
7. Sol III
8. 89.7 pounds (Earth weight times the gravitational effect of Altair IV)
9. The animals shown would not have had that exact form 200,000 years ago, and would have changed during that time.
10. A neutron beam would be a stream of neutron particles. It could be dangerous if it penetrated tissue.
11. Looking into a mirror that faced a reactor would be dangerous because the viewer's back would receive radiation from the reactor.

Parts of a nuclear power plant:

1. E
2. G
3. A
4. B
5. F
6. D
7. C

Personal Radiation Dose

We live in a radioactive world. Radiation is all around us as part of our natural environment. It is measured in terms of *millirems*(mrems). The annual average dose per person from all sources is about 360 mrems, but it is not uncommon for any of us to receive far more than that in a given year (usually due to medical procedures). For those who work with nuclear materials the international standards allow up to 5,000 mrems a year exposure.

Where you live

Cosmic radiation at sea level (from outer space)	26
For your elevation (in feet): 3 mrems for every 1000 feet	_____
Terrestrial (from ground)	
If you live in a state that border the Gulf or Atlantic add 23	
If you live in the Colorado Plateau Area add 90	
If you live in Middle America add 46	_____
House construction:	
If you live in a stone, brick or concrete building add 7	_____

What you eat and drink

Internal radiation (in your body)	
From food and water U.S. average	40
From air (radon) U.S. average	200

How you live *(use information from the past year only)*

Weapons test fallout (less than 1)	1
Jet plane travel:	
For each 1000 miles you travel add 1	_____
If you have porcelain crowns or false teeth add 0.07	_____
If you use gas lantern mantels when camping add 0.003	_____
If you wear a luminous wristwatch (LCD) add 0.06	_____
If you use luggage inspection at airports (typical X-ray machines) add 0.002	_____
If you use a video display terminal (less than 0.1) add 1	_____
TV viewing: For each hour per day _____ x 0.15=	_____
If you have a smoke detector add 0.008	_____
If you wear a plutonium-powered cardiac pacemaker add 100	_____
If you have had medical exposures	
Chest X-rays add 10 per visit	_____
Gastrointestinal tract X-ray 200 per visit	_____
Dental X-rays 10 per visit	_____
If you have had nuclear medical procedures (U.S. average: add 14)	_____
If you live within 50 miles of a nuclear power plant (U.S. average: add 0.0009)	_____
If you live within 50 miles of a coal-fired electrical utility plant add 0.03	_____
If you smoke add 1300	_____

One mrem per year is equal to: Moving to an elevation 100 feet higher
Increasing your diet by 4%; Taking a 4 day vacation in the Sierra Nevada Mountains; The radiation you receive from sitting next to a person for an hour a day

Past Year'sTotal:

Size of the Sun & Moon

It's possible to measure the size of the sun or moon by the size of an image created from the light of that object. If you know the distance to the the sun or moon and the size of the image created then you can calculate the real size of the object.   By using a pinhole and a screen you can project the image of any bright object. Then use the following formula method to calculate size.

$$\frac{\text{diameter of sun (or moon)}}{\text{distance of sun (or moon) to earth}} = \frac{\text{diameter of image}}{\text{distance of spot from pinhole}}$$

It is important to measure as closely as possible the size of the image.
The distance from the Earth to the Sun is about 93,000,000 miles
The distance from the Earth to the Moon is about 239,000 miles.

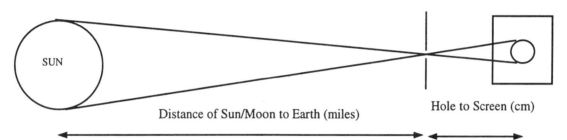

Distance of Sun/Moon to Earth (miles)   Hole to Screen (cm)

Materials:
Paper Towel Tube,   Wax Paper
Aluminum Foil,   Ruler,   Pin
Procedure:
Cut out a square of wax paper and Al foil about 10 cm. by 10 cm. Using a pin make parallel scratchs near the center of the wax paper. Make 11 marks,
0.1 cm. (1mm) apart. Tape the wax paper, with the marks in the center on one end of the paper towel tube and tape the Al foil onto the other end. Carefully poke a hole in the center of the Al foil.
Point the foil end of the tube at the sun (or moon) and adjust until an image forms on the wax paper where the scratches were made. Carefully measure the size of the image.

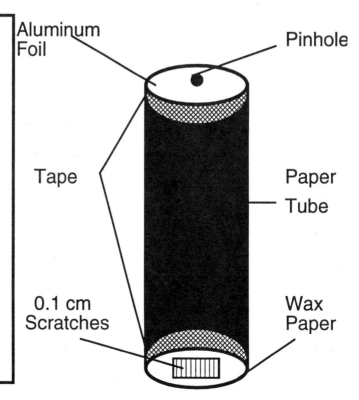

Data & Calculations for Sun & Moon Size

Data: Sun

Length of Tube (cm.) = _____

Size of Sun's Image (cm.) = _____

Distance to Sun (miles) = _____

Calculation:

size of sun = distance to sun X diameter of image
                        length of tube

Size of Sun (miles)=_____

Data: Moon

Length of Tube (cm.) = _____

Size of Moon's Image (cm.) = _____

Distance to Moon (miles) = _____

Calculation:

size of moon = distance to moon X diameter of image
                          length of tube

Size of Moon (miles)=_____

Percent Error: If you know the actual amount of what you are trying to measure then you can calculate the percent error of your measurement. The percent error is the difference between your answer and the actual answer, compared to the actual amount. Look up the actual sizes of the sun and moon.
Use the formula:

$$\frac{(actual - measured)}{(actual)} \times 100 = \quad \%$$

Percent Error for Sun = _____ Percent Error for Moon = _____

Free Fall and Forces

Materials:

2 disk shaped magnets with holes
(holes should be large enough to allow
magnets to go onto dowel)
1 small dowel or pen body
Small circle of cardboard
Clear plastic drink bottle
Nail (to punch hole in bottle)

     It is often difficult to observe the
behavior of objects, because they are
influenced by forces that cannot be seen,
such as gravity. To study the behavior
of an object it may be necessary to
isolate it as much as possible.
     The local effects of gravity on an
object can be temporarily eliminated by
placing the object in a state of **Free Fall.**
During free fall the object falls in the
Earth's gravitational field with an
acceleration equal to that due to the
Earth's gravity (neglecting air friction).
So while in free fall, objects seem to
have no weight relative to each other.
As the object falls, since there is no
force to counteract the object's weight,
the object experiences *"weightlessness."*
This is what happens to astronauts as
they fall (orbit) around the Earth.
     During this activity you will
make observations of objects in a state
of free fall and see the effects of
weightlessness.

Free Fall Magnets

Procedure:

1. Glue or thumbtack the cardboard circle onto the
   end of the dowel.
2. Place the two magnets onto the dowel so that the
   magnets are repelling each other. (like poles next to
   each other)
3. Hold the dowel in an upright or vertical position
   and observe the behavior of the magnets. (see
   vertical magnet diagram)
4. Release the apparatus allowing it to fall about two
   to three feet
   (1 meter) and try to observe what happens to the
   magnets as they fall.
5. Replace the two magnets onto the dowel as before
   (step 2).
6. Hold the dowel in a sideways or horizontal
   position and observe the behavior of the magnets.
   (see horizontal magnet diagram)
4. Release the apparatus allowing it to fall about two
   to three feet
   (1 meter) and try to observe what happens to the
   magnets as they fall.

*Repeat the above steps as necessary to get the
observations.*

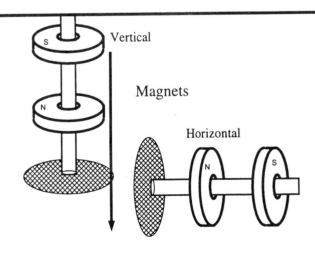

Vertical

Magnets

Horizontal

Free Fall Fluids

Procedure: (do outside in a clear area)

1. Using a nail poke a hole in the side (near the bottom) of a clear plastic drink bottle.
2. Covering the hole with your finger, fill the bottle with water.
3. Hold the bottle in an upright or vertical position. Remove your finger from the hole and observe the behavior of the fluid.
4. Release the apparatus allowing it to fall about two to three feet (1 meter) and try to observe what happens to the fluid as it falls.
5. Refill the bottle as before (step 2).
6. Hold the bottle upright and observe the behavior of the fluid.
4. Throw the bottle up into the air (try not to spin the bottle) and observe the behavior of the fluid as the bottle rises, stops, and then falls.

Repeat the above steps as often as necessary to get the observations.

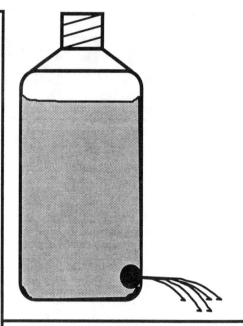

A Free Fall Question:

Why should you avoid spinning any of the objects in this activity? (hint: makes what force?)

Observations Data Table

	In the Earth's Gravity Field	In Free Fall
Vertical Magnets		
Horizontal Magnets		
Dropped Bottle		
Tossed Bottle		

Parallax Viewing

Materials:
- scissors
- thread
- glue stick
- pin

Parallax involves the looking at an object from two different positions (angles). People see depth as a result of stereo vision where objects are looked at from two slightly different positions. Each eye sees from a slightly different perspective, and the brain then combines these two images to form a three dimensional picture. You can see how his works if you hold up a finger at arms length, and then alternately close one eye and then the other. You should notice that the background past your finger shifts as you change eyes, this is an effect of parallax.

In astronomy parallax is used to locate near (astronomically speaking) objects and it is also used to measure distances. To produce the best parallax image the two viewpoints should be as far apart as possible, so astronomers take photographs of a section of the night sky six months apart (opposite ends of the Earth's orbit). Then by measuring angles and knowing the width of the Earth's orbit it is possible to calculate the distance from the Earth to an object. You can also use the photographic images to locate nearby objects, such as planets, comets, and asteroids. The two common methods for locating nearby objects using photographs are stereo scanning and blink comparator.

Stereo Scanning

Stereo scanning creates a stereooptical illusion. Below are simplified diagrams of starfield pictures. The two pictures may seem identical, but they aren't. To find the planetoid in the picture what you have to do is called stereopisis, have your brain superimpose the two pictures (one for each eye) into one image.

1. Cut off the lower section of the page.
2. Hold the diagrams at arms length.
3. Relax your eyes to a soft focus, don't try to keep the pictures in perfect focus.
4. Slowly bring the picture closer until a third, superimposed image becomes visible in the center. This image will appear identical to the outer images except that any point that is different will seem to float off into a different visual plane.
5. By noticing which point has shifted and identifying its location on each diagram, you located the nearby planetoid.

Blink Comparator

When using a device called the blink comparator, a light is blinked on and off, switching between two starfield photographs. Each photo is viewed for just a moment, but the blinking goes so fast that the image appears continuous, similar to how a motion picture seems continuous (even though it is just a series of still pictures).

Any nearby object will appear to jump back and forth, while the background stars will appear fixed.

1. Make a blink thaumatrope by cutting out the pictures below and gluing them back to back. The pictures should be glued on so that one picture is upside down compared to the other, and the crosses must line up exactly with each other.
2. With a pin poke holes in the + marks and attach a two inch loop of string through each of the holes.
3. Grasping the ends of each string slowly spin the card by rolling the string between the thumb and index finger to create the blinking effect to find the planetoid.

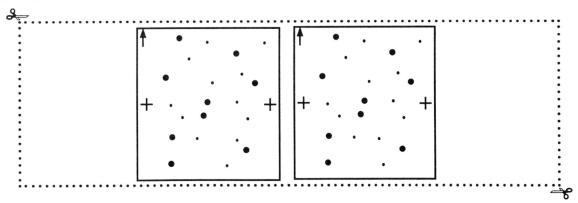

More parallax pictures to scan

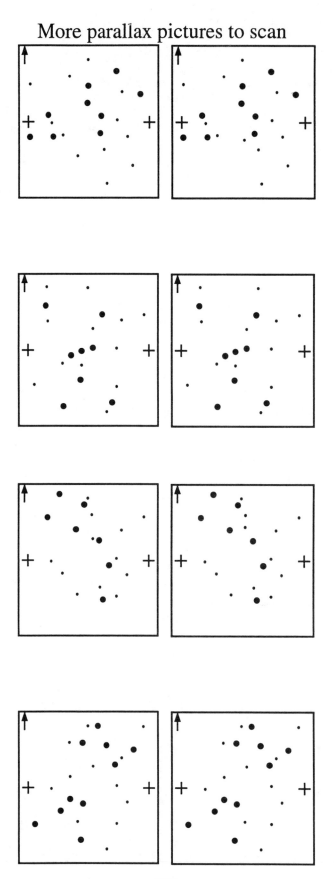

202

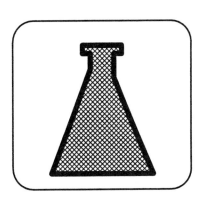

STS: Science Technology & Society:

Day the Earth Stood Still
Devil in the Dark
Ethics

Activity:
Build an Electric Motor

DAY THE EARTH STOOD STILL
Teacher Information

Content Areas:
Forms of energy, technology: radar; electricity, speed, velocity, laws of motion, robotics.

Synopsis:
A spaceship lands in a park in Washington D.C. A person (Klaatu) and a robot emerge. The army overreacting, shoots the person, who is then taken to a hospital. Then Klaatu escapes and goes out among humanity to learn about people. He enlists the aid of a local scientist in gathering scientists from around the world, so that he can give them a message for humanity. To get people's attention, Klaatu stops electricity all over the world. In the end Klaatu delivers the message to humanity to live in peace or be destroyed by the robot police.

Good Science:
Mr. Carpenter's definition of Inertia is correct.
The speeds shown by the spaceship are possible.

Bad Science:
There is no known inhabited planet within the distance described.
It would not be possible to selectively turn off (stop) electricity world wide.
It is implausible that the beam weapon would destroy only weapons and not people.

THE DAY THE EARTH STOOD STILL

Directed by Robert Wise   First shown in 1951
Black & White   92 minutes,
Based on the novelette "Farewell to the Master" by Harry Bates
(Gort: Klaatu Barada Nikto)

Questions to be answered during the video:

1. What is the speed of the object being tracked by radar?

2. In what city does the ship land?

3. "The ship is designed for travel outside the _____"

4. What happens to Klaatu after he takes an object from his suit?

5. What was the object?

6. To get to Earth Klaatu traveled _____months and

   _____miles

7. The doctors looking at Klaatu's X-rays say that he is _____.

8. What has happened to the bullet wound?

9. When Klaatu gets out of the hospital, where does the newspaper say he is from?(what planet)

10. The radio describes Klaatu as _____

11. What reasons does Klaatu/Carpenter give for using diamonds for money?

12. What does Klaatu/Carpenter say is the power source of the space ship?

13. What is the property of matter that remains in uniform motion unless acted upon by an
    outside force?

14. What behavior does Professor Barnhart say makes good science?

15. Klaatu/Carpenter has brought a warning because Earth now has what two things?

16. What is Bobby's mother's reaction to Bobby saying he saw Mr. Carpenter go into the
    spaceship?

17. What is Klaatu/Carpenter's demonstration of power to the world?

18. In what has the robot (Gort) been encased?

19. Why does Tom turn in Klaatu/Carpenter to the military?

20. What does the military do to Klaatu/Carpenter?

21. What does Gort do to Klaatu in the ship?

22. Gort is a member of a race of robots that act as _____.

23.What is the Earth's choice?

The Day the Earth Stood Still: Vocabulary

1. Alternative   2. Atomic   3. Electricity   4. Experiment
5. Inertia   6. Media   7. Neutralize   8. Radar
9. Robot   10. Speed of Sound   11. Supersonic   12. Tracking

The Day the Earth Stood Still: Discussion questions

1. If it took Klaatu 5 months to travel 250 million miles, what was his speed in miles per hour?

2. What rules or limits do you think would be necessary if robots were to act as police?

3. Describe how the media was portrayed in the movie. How do you think that media reports on science?

4. In the movie other "people" had come to Earth to "complain" about our new technology. This does happen between countries and states on Earth. What do you think would be the impact of a new technology (constructive and destructive) if a
   a) new source of fuel were found?   b) new type of television were marketed?
   c) new type of computer were discovered?   d) way to genetically engineer plants?

5. Dependence of people on electricity: (energy web). We use electricity all the time around us, sometimes obviously, sometimes not so obviously. Trace the types of energy used and figure out where (and if) electricity comes into play.

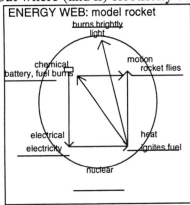

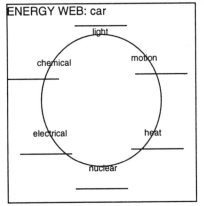

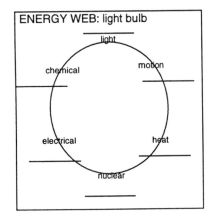

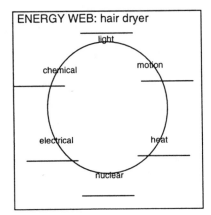

6. Map of the solar system: find Klaatu's planet

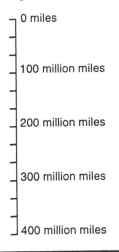

0 miles

100 million miles

200 million miles

300 million miles

400 million miles

First label the six planets of the
solar system on the diagram
(the Earth is already marked).
Then using a compass
draw a circle 250 million miles
in radius around the Earth's
position. Then list the planets
that Klaatu could be from.

Klaatu's Possible Planets

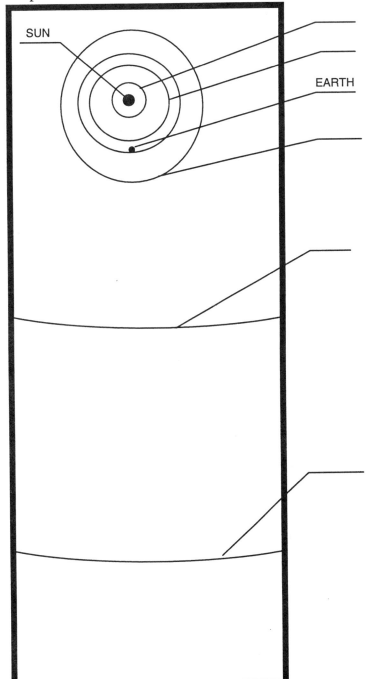

SUN

EARTH

The Day the Earth Stood Still: Answers to video questions

1. 4000 miles per hour
2. Washington, DC, USA
3. atmosphere
4. he opens it and gets shot
5. a gift to allow the study life on other planets
6. 5 months and 250 million miles
7. normal, human
8. has healed overnight
9. "Man from Mars"
10. a Monster or Menace
11. easier to carry and they don't wear out
12. atomic energy
13. inertia
14. curiosity
15. atomic weapons and rockets
16. he was having a dream
17. all electricity has been neutralized for 1/2 of an hour
18. a plastic (KL93)
19. so he can get his picture in the paper/be important
20. shoots him dead
21. brings him back to life
22. police
23. join in peace or be destroyed

The Day the Earth Stood Still: Suggested discussion answers

1. About 70,000 mi/hr.
2. Answers will vary.
3. Answers will vary.
4. Answers will vary.
5.   car: chemical (gas) -> heat (combustion) -> motion (car moving)
       light bulb: nuclear (power plant) or chemical (coal/oil)-> electrical -> heat/light (light)
       hair dryer: nuclear/chemical (power plant) -> electrical -> heat (hot air)
6. Any of the inner planets (Mercury, Venus, Mars) are within the distance.

Star Trek®: DEVIL IN THE DARK
Teacher Information

Content Areas:
Organic chemistry, chemistry of life, inorganic chemistry, property of matter, behavior of elements, acids, materials sciences, nuclear power, mining, endangered species, loss of habitat.

Synopsis:
The crew of the Enterprise, while on a mining planet, encounters a new lifeform. The silicon based (inorganic) lifeform fighting back against threats to its eggs, attempts to destroy all the people. Upon discovering that the silicon life form is intelligent, people make a pact with it and learn to coexist.

Good Science:
The chemical properties of elements are presented correctly.
Silicon does have many of the properties of silicon (same family).
All life known is based on carbon compounds.
Most acids do react exothermically, producing heat.

Bad Science:
There is no known way for a matter transporter system to work.
There is no known way to travel or communicate faster than light.
There is no such element as purgeium.

StarTrek®: THE DEVIL IN THE DARK

Episode 26   Airdate March 9, 1967
Color   51 minutes
StarTrek and Chemistry

Questions to be answered during the video:

1. How was Shmiter killed?

2. What kind of planet is Janus 6?

3. When was a new level opened?

4. What had happened to the machine metals?

5. How does Ed describe the monster?

6. Of what material is the silver sphere that Spock is holding made?

7. What does McCoy say that the man cause of death?

8. What is the warning on the power reactor?

9. What is missing from the reactor that will cause it to go supercritical?

10. Why don't shut down the reactor?

11. Life as we know it is based on what kind of compounds?

12. What other element is suggested as a life base?

13. Silicon based life is impossible when living in what kind of atmosphere?

14. When did the creature first appear?

15. At which level were the nodules of silicon found?

16. The creature seems made of fibrous asbestos -- which is what kind of material?

17. What can the creature's body excrete?

18. Why does Spock not want the creature killed?

19. What are the odds of both Spock and Kirk being killed?

20. Why does Spock now want the creature killed?

21. What does the creature write on the rock?

22. Why is this statement confusing?

23. Of what material is the creature made?

24. What are the silicon nodules?

25. The Horta's entire race dies out every _____ years?

26. The Horta are the greatest natural _____ in existence?

27. How does McCoy fix the Horta?

28. What elements does Chief Vandenburg state they have found?

Devil in the Dark: Vocabulary

1. Acid	2. Agent	3. Base	4. Bearing
5. Colony	6. Corrosive	7. Element	8. Excrete
9. Mineral	10. Nodule	11. Ore	12. Radiation
13. Radius	14. Rare Earth Elements	15. Reactor	16. Volcanic

Devil in the Dark: Discussion questions

1. Compare Silicon to Carbon on a periodic chart. What do they have in common?

2. What is the electron configuration diagram for silicon and carbon?

3. How do metals act in the presence of an acid?

4. What is the chemical formula for asbestos?

5. Purgeium is a fictitious element: make up an atomic number, atomic mass and symbol for this element.

6. What is your opinion of Spock's choice to try to have the creature captured because it is an endangered species?

Devil in the Dark: Answers to video questions

1. burned to death
2. mining
3. 6 months ago
4. corroded
5. shaggy
6. silicon
7. acid burns
8. radiation
9. pump part
10. needed for life support
11. carbon
12. silicon
13. oxygen
14. 6 months ago
15. lowest
16. mineral
17. corrosive acid
18. last of its kind
19. a whole lot to one
20. endangering the Capt.
21. NO KILL I
22. no punctuation
23. silicon/rock
24. eggs
25. 50,000 years
26. miners
27. cement/concrete
28. Ni, Mo, Au, Pt, and rare earths

Devil in the Dark: Suggested discussion answers

1. Members of the same family (Carbon Family) and therfore have similar chemical properties and the same number of electrons in their outter shell (4 valence electrons).

2.   Si: $1s^2\ 2s^2\ 2p^4\ 3s^2\ 3p^2$

   C: $1s^2\ 2s^2\ 2p^2$

3. Most metals will react with a strong acid to produce hydrogen gas and a salt. (but not all).
4. Asbestos is a silicate of magnesium, Mg_2SiO_4
5. Answers will vary.
6. Answers will vary.

Star Trek: The Next Generation®: ETHICS
Teacher Information

Content Areas:
Medical ethics, medical technology, physiology, risk assessment.

Synopsis:
After an accident injuring his spine, Whorf must decide on whether to risk experimental surgery or survive with limited mobility. Emotionally unable to accept limited mobility, he chooses the experimental surgery. Only his alien physiology of redundant systems allows him to survive the surgery.

Good Science:
The descriptions of spine structure and functions are correct.
The questions of procedures for medical experimentation discussed in the film are often
        discussed among professionals today.

Bad Science:
There is no known way for a matter transporter system to work.
There is no known way to travel or communicate faster than light.
It is not currently possible to transplant spines.

Star Trek: The Next Generation®: ETHICS

Episode 216   *Air Date: 3/2/92*
Color   *46 minutes*
A question of who is right

Questions to be answered during the video.

1. What happens to Whorf when he and Geordi are searching?

2. What is wrong with Whorf's back?

3. What kind of specialist is Dr. Russell?

4. Dr. Crusher believes Whorf's _____ to be permanent.

5. Whorf wants Riker to help him perform Hup Pa, to help him _____.

6. Whorf's _____ has begun to deteriorate.

7. Klingons have redundant systems and a different physiology. They have:

   _____ ribs   _____ livers   _____ chambered heart

8. Which of Whorf's parts can the replicator replace?

9. What happened to the other ship, the Denver?

10. Why can't Alexander see his father?

11. What kind of injuries are Dr. Russell's speciality?

12. The devices will give Whorf how much of his mobility? _____%

13. Why did the Doctor say the Perozine couldn't be used?

14. Dr. Crusher disagrees with Dr. Russell's methods and has her relieved of_____

15. What is the first tenet of good medicine?

16. What is Dr. Russell doing to the brain stem and spinal column?

17. What does Dr. Russell have to scan manually, because her machine is having problems?

18. The tissue is growing at anticipated rates and there is no initial sign of _____

19. What is happening to the synapses' response?

20. When did death occur?

21. What do Klingons have for their synaptic systems?

22. Dr. Crusher says that good research takes _____.

Ethics: Vocabulary

1. Brain stem
2. Ethics
3. Ganglia
4. Neurospecialist
5. Paralysis
6. Physiology
7. Redundant
8. Rejection
9. Research
10. Spinal cord
11. Spine
12. Synapse

Ethics: Discussion questions

1. Is it more important to try and do the best for the individual or to experiment to help the larger population?

2. Should medical research be done on people who have terminal diseases?

3. Should medical research be done on people who cannot speak for themselves?

4. Would you rather lose some of your abilities or have a very risky treatment?

5. Is quality of life an important consideration for someone with a debilitating problem?

6. What is a living will for?

7. Match and label the parts of the brain:

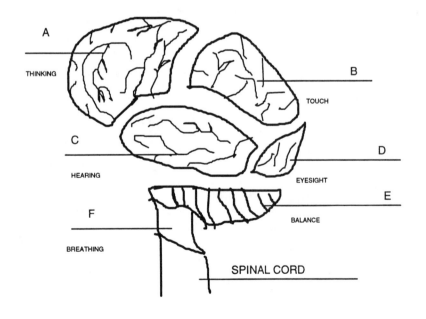

1. CEREBELLUM
2. FRONTAL LOBE
3. MEDULLA
4. OCCIPITAL LOBE
5. PARIETAL LOBE
6. TEMPORAL LOBE

Ethics: Answers to video questions
1. a container falls on his back
2. spine is crushed
3. neurospecialist
4. paralysis
5. commit suicide
6. synapse function
7. 20 ribs
   2 livers
   8 chambered heart
8. spine
9. hit a mine and crashed
10. pride, his father does not want himself seen in his state
11. spinal
12. 60%
13. blood pressure too high
14. all duties
15. not to make the patient any worse
16. separating
17. ganglia
18. rejection
19. failing
20. 2024
21. a redundant system
22. time

Ethics: Suggested discussion answers
1. Answers will vary.
2. Answers will vary.
3. Answers will vary.
4. Answers will vary.
5. Answers will vary.
6. To provide others with information about what a patient wants done to himself/herself when he/she can no longer communicate.
7. 1-E, 2-A, 3-F, 4-D 5-C 6-B

Build an Electric Motor

An electric motor works off the interplay between electricity and magnetism. An electric current (of electrons) flows from the battery through the wire. A moving electric charge produces a magnetic field that surrounds the wire where the charges are moving. This effect is called electromagnetism. In an electric motor we use a coil of wire instead of a straight wire because with coils the magnetic effect of each loop adds to the magnetic field. The magnetic field produced by the coil interacts with a permenant magnetic field of another magnet and produces forces that cause the coil to move. Magnets react with each other in that similar magnetic fields repel each other and opposite magnetic fields attract each other. With the enamel stripped off of one side of the wire, as the coil spins, the electricity in the coil is turned on and off, and also turning on and off the magnetic field.

Materials:
1 D-cell battery
2 large paperclips
6 feet of #20 to
   #25 enameled
   wire
Tape

1. Make the coil: wrap the wire 20 to 25 times in a circle about 1 inch in diameter, leave about 2 inches sticking out on each side.

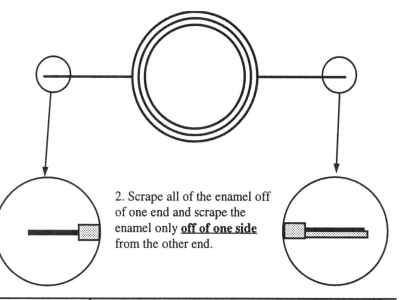

2. Scrape all of the enamel off of one end and scrape the enamel only **off of one side** from the other end.

3. Bend the 2 paperclips in the following manner. Bend the inside section up and flat with the outside section. Then pull the smaller free end over to make a loop.

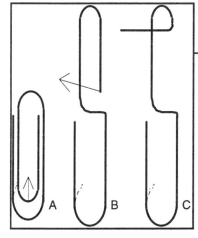

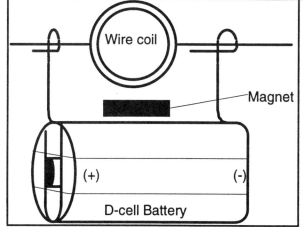

4. Assemble your motor as shown. Tape the paperclips on each end parallel to each other, place the coil into the paperclips, and place the magnet under the coil. Start the motor spinning. It should turn by itself, but you may need to adjust the magnet's positon.

Glossary

Definitions of the vocabulary words used as they relate to the films.

Aftershock .... An earthquake of lesser intensity that occurs after the main quake.
Alternative .... Another choice or possibility.
Accelerate .... To change speed, to go faster.
Accuracy .... Correctness.
Acid .... A chemical that contains hydronium (H+) ions
Aft .... Rear or back.
Agent .... A substance that can cause or take part in a reaction.
Alimentary canal .... A tube leading from the mouth to the anus.
Amber .... Fossilized tree sap.
Amino acid .... Molecules that make up proteins.
Amoeba .... A single celled animal.
Amplifier .... A machine used to increase a signal.
Android .... A machine that has the appearance of a human.
Andromeda .... A galaxy very similar in structure to our own.
Antenna .... A sense organ on the head of an insect.
Antibody .... Chemicals which kill foreign material inside the body.
Appendicitis .... Inflammation of the appendix.
Appropriation .... Money set aside for a specific use.
Arable .... Land that can be used for farming.
Artery .... A blood vessel that transports blood away from the heart.
Astronomer .... A person who studies astronomy
Atomic .... Refers to the atom, the smallest particle with the properties of an element.
Atomic bomb .... An explosion caused by the fission of atoms.
Auxiliary .... To give help or support.

Bacteria .... Single cell organism with no nucleus.
Baleen .... A type of whale that filters its food.
Barricade .... A temporary barrier.
Base .... A chemical that contains hydroxide (OH-) ions
Bearing .... A compass heading.
Biologist .... A person who studies biology
Biped .... Having two legs.
Bisexual .... A living thing having characteristics of both sexes.
Blowhole .... A hole in a whale's head used for breathing.
Botanist .... A person who studies plants.
Botany .... The study of plants.
Brain stem .... The part of the brain that connects to the spine.

Capillary .... The smallest type of blood vessel.
Carbon .... An element composed of 6 protons, 6 neutrons and 6 electrons.

Carnivore ....A plant or animal that uses other animals for food.
Cartilage.............................A flexible connective tissue.
Catalyst ....A material that causes a chemical reaction to occur or speed up, when it normally would not.
Cavity................................A hole or hollow space.
Cell...................................Basic organizational unit of life.
Cephalopod.........................Class of molluscs with tentacles.
Cetacean.............................An order of aquatic mammals that includes whales.
Chain reaction.....................A series in which each event causes the next event to occur.
Chaos ....The mathematical study of the lack of order.
Chitin ....The hard material that makes outer body shell of an insect.
Chromosome.......................The structures inside a cell containing the genetic code.
Cinnabar............................An ore usually bright red to brownish red containing mercury and sulfur.
Claustrophobia....................Fear of inclosed places.
Cleavage ....The manner in which a rock breaks or splits in a certain direction.
Clone.................................To reproduce from a single cell by asexual reproduction.
Clot ....A material that has solidified.
Colony..............................A group of similar organisms living close together.
Coma................................A state of prolonged unconsciousness.
Combustion........................A chemical reaction involving the addition of oxygen.
Compound ....A material made up of two or more different kinds of atoms.
Conductor (elect.) ....A material that can easily carry electricity.
Conservation......................To preserve or save.
Core ....The center section of the Earth.
Corpuscle ....A blood cell.
Corrosive ....Eating or wearing away by reaction.
Cortex ....The bark of a tree.
Crust.................................The outer solid layer of the Earth.
Crystal..............................A material made up of atoms in a regular pattern forming a shape.

Density..............................The mass of an object divided by its volume.
Deterrent ....Something that discourages or stops.
Dinosaur............................An extinct group of reptiles.
Disease..............................A condition of ill health.
Dissect ....To cut in pieces.
Dissolve ....To suspend one material into another in a liquid state.
DNA.................................Genetic material that makes up chromosomes.
Dormant............................A state of inactivity.
Drone ....A worker insect.
Dynamic............................Actively changing.

Earthquake.........................A sudden disruption in the Earth's crust.
Ego..................................The mental representation of self.
Electricity..........................A force dealing with the flow of electrons.

Element...........................A material composed of only one type of atom.
Embryo ....An organism in its earliest stage of development.
Entomologist....................A person who studies insects.
Environment ....The conditions and materials that make up the surroundings.
Epilepsy ....A nervous system disease.
Escape velocity ....The speed necessary to leave a planetary body and not return.
Ethics ....Moral principles and rules of conduct.
Evacuate.........................To remove material and to make empty.
Evolution ....The steps a species goes through to adapt to the environment.
Excrete...........................To discharge or expel from a body
Exotic.............................A non-native species.
Expedition.......................A trip made for a specific purpose.
Experiment......................The scientific process of learning by observing.
Extinct...........................When all of a species no longer exists.

Factor ....A contributing cause or a number which when multiplied gives a
                                 certain result.
Fatal ....To cause death.
Fault..............................A crack in the rock material where movement has occurred.
Flipper...........................The forward limbs on a marine mammal.
Fluke ....The tail of a whale.
Follicle...........................A small space or gland.
Force ....A push or pull.
Fossil.............................Evidence of past life.
Frequency.......................The number of repeated occurrences in a specific amount of time.
Fusion ....The union of atoms.

Ganglia...........................The main body of the nerve cell.
Geiger counter ....A machine used to detect radiation.
Gene..............................Part of a cell that contains heredity information.
Generator ....A machine that takes in one form of energy and converts it into
                                 another from.
Genetic...........................Having to do with genes or heredity
Genetic Engineering ....The process by which people change the structure of genes.
Geologist.........................A person who studies geology.
Geriatric.........................The study and treatment of old age.
Glare ....A reflection of light off of a surface.
Gravity ....The attractive force common to all mass.
Greenhouse ....A glass house in which plants are grown.

Habitat ....The natural home for a living thing.
Harpoon ....A type of spear used for fishing and whaling.
Herbivore........................An animal that only eats plants.
Hibernating ....When an animal's system becomes inactive because of its
                                 environment.

Host...................................The organism upon which a parasite feeds.
Hybrid...............................A crossbreed or offspring of different varieties living things.
Hydraulic ....Applications of the motions of liquids.
Hysteria.............................Violent emotional outbreaks.

Id......................................The mental representation of the urge for pleasure.
Immunity...........................Protection from a disease,
Impulse (physics)...............A thrusts or push to cause change in movement.
Inert..................................Being inactive.
Inertia...............................The property of matter to continue moving in the same speed and
                                            direction unless acted on by an outside force.
Infection............................To be affected by a disease.
Inflammation.....................Swelling on the body.
Ingest................................To eat.
Inorganic ....Non-organic (not containing carbon)
Insecticide ....An insect poison.
Ionized ....To become electrically charged.
Isotope...............................An atom with a different number of neutrons than the standard.

Laceration ....A cut or tear.
Laser ....A device that emits light of only one wavelength.
Lateral...............................Related to the side.
Lava ....Liquid rock on the earth's surface.
Lethal ....To cause death.
Life....................................Anything having the ability to assimilate, reproduce, and move.
Limestone ....A type of sedimentary rock composed of calcium carbonate.
Litter ....Offspring born at one time.
Locust ....A type of grasshopper.
Lymphatic system ....The system in the body that fights disease.

Magma...............................Liquid rock under the earth's surface.
Magnetometer.....................A tool used to detect magnetic fields.
Mammal.............................An warm blooded animal that bears live young and produces milk.
Mantle...............................A layer of the Earth found under the crust.
Media.................................Any way of communicating information.
Metabolism ....The chemical process of absorbing food.
Meteor...............................Matter from space that heats up from friction with the Earth's
                                            atmosphere and glows.
Microbe.............................A germ or bacteria.
Microorganism....................A microscopic living thing.
Mineral..............................Any naturally occurring material found in the Earth's crust.
Miniaturize........................To make smaller.
Mixture ....Two or more different chemicals together, but not reacting with each
                                            other.
Model................................A representation of something real, used for experimentation.

Monolith .... A large single stone.
Mutate .... To change genetically.

Nervous system .... The body system that receives and transmits information.
Neuron .... A single nerve cell.
Neurospecialist .... A person who studies the nervous system.
Neutralize .... To make inactive.
Nodule .... A small lump of material.
Nucleus .... The controlling part of a cell.

Octopus .... A marine mollusk with eight limbs and no shell.
Optic .... Having to do with light.
Orbit .... The circular path of one object around another object.
Ore .... A mineral that contains some worthwhile material.
Organic .... Having to do with living materials.
Organism .... A living thing.
Oscilloscope .... A machine used to study waves

Paralysis .... The inability to move.
Parasite .... An organism that lives in or on another organism.
Parsec .... A unit of great distance, equal to about 3.25 light years.
Pestilence .... A disease having devastating effects.
Petrified .... To turn to stone.
pH .... A scale used to measure the strength of acids and bases.
Phase .... A state of matter.
Photoelectric .... The process in which light energy is converted into electrical energy.
Physiology .... Having to do with the processes of living.
Pitch .... A particular frequency.
Plane (surface) .... A flat or level surface.
Plasma .... An electrified gas.
Poison .... A harmful chemical.
Porous .... Containing holes, a material that allows another material to flow
                                            through it.
Predator .... An animal that hunts other animals.
Predict .... To forecast.
Prey .... An animal that is hunted by other animals.
Probe .... A tool used to gather information.
Production .... The act of making.
Prolific .... Producing young abundantly.
Propaganda .... Information given in support of only one view.
Protoplasm .... The liquid part of a cell.
Prototype .... The first one of a kind made.
Puncture .... To put a hole into.
Pupil .... The dark circle in the eye that lets light in.

Quarantine ....To separate or isolate for health reasons.
Queen.................................The dominant female insect.

Radar.................................A method of radio detection which detects objects by the reflection of radio waves.
Radiation...........................The emission of energy through space by particles or waves.
Radius ....The distance or line from the center to the edge of a circle.
Raptor ....Any bird of prey.
Rare Earth Elements ....Any of the following elements: Sc, Y, La, Ce, Pr, Nd, Pm, Sm, Eu, Gd, Tb, Dy, Ho, Er, Tm, Yb, Lu.
Reaction mass....................The material used in a reaction to cause motion to occur.
Reactor..............................A device in which controlled nuclear chain reactions occur.
Red Blood Cell ....The type of blood cell that carries oxygen.
Redundant..........................A duplicated system for use as backup in case the first system fails.
Reflex................................An involuntary reaction.
Regenerate ....To grow or form again.
Rejection...........................To refuse to accept.
Reproduction ....The process of generating offspring.
Reptile...............................A cold blooded scaled lunged animal.
Research............................To study or investigate.
Respiratory........................Having to do with breathing.
Richter Scale.....................A scale used to measure earthquakes, each number on the scale is ten times stronger than the number before it.
Risk...................................The amount of danger or hazard.
Robot ....A self guiding machine.
Rocket...............................A projectile propelled by self contained fuel.
Rogue................................A solitary animal.

Sabotage............................To willfully destroy or interfere with.
Saline ....A solution that contains salt (NaCl).
Secrete ....To produce a substance by glandular activity.
Sedated.............................Medically or chemically soothed or calmed.
Seismic.............................Earthquake or earthquake related.
Seismograph ....A machine used to measure the strength of earthquakes.
Serrate..............................Having sharp teeth.
Shelter..............................A protective area.
Silhouette ....The appearance of an object as it is lit from behind.
Simulation.........................The process of imitating something.
Solution.............................When one material has been dissolved into another material.
SONAR..............................A method of detection which detects objects by the reflection of sound waves.
Sounding...........................A measurement of depth.
Species ....An group of organisms separate and distinct from others.
Spectrograph ....A tool used to measure different wavelengths of light.
Spectrum...........................All of the wavelengths of light.

230

Speed ....Distance divided by time.
Speed of Sound...................Rate at which sound travels (333 m/s)
Spinal cord..........................The nerve tissue found in the backbone.
Spine...................................The backbone
Squid...................................A marine mollusk with 8 limbs and an internal shell.
Stalactite ....A cave rock formation that hangs from the ceiling.
Stalagmite ....A cave rock formation that forms on cave floors.
Stimulant.............................Anything that causes body systems to speed up.
Supersonic ....Moving faster than the speed of sound.
Symmetrical........................Being equal on both sides.
Symptom..............................A sign or signal of disease.
Synapse ....The fluid filled space between nerve cells.
Synthetic ....Artificial, man made.

Tactical ....Having to do with strategy and planning.
Tektite.................................Rocks formed from the impact of meteors with the Earth.
Territoriality........................An organism behavior in relation to its region.
Theory.................................A scientific guess.
Thorax.................................The central body part of an animal.
Thrust..................................A pushing force.
Tissue..................................A group of cells acting together for a similar function.
Trace ....A small but measurable amount.
Tracking..............................To follow or trace a course of motion.
Tranquilizer ....A drug used to slow down body systems.
Trench (oceanic) ....A long narrow crevice.
Tsunami (tidal wave)...........A seismic sea wave, a large wave caused by an earthquake.
Turbulence ....The movement of a disturbed fluid.

Ultrasonic............................(Supersonic) faster than the speed of sound.
Ultraviolet...........................The section of the spectrum above human sight.

Vacuum................................Absence of matter.
Vector ....A method of describing a unit with direction.
Velocity...............................Speed with direction.
Virus ....A microscopic agent of infection or disease.
Volcanic..............................Having to do with volcanoes.
Volcano...............................A vent in the Earth's surface from which molten rock can flow.

Water Table ....The upper surface of water under the ground.
Wave...................................A disturbance within a medium.
White Blood Cell.................A disease fighting cell.
Wound ....An injury to tissue.

Xenon..................................A chemical element, symbol Xe having 54 protons, 78 neutrons, and 54 electrons.